Instant Pot for Two Cookbook

205 Easy, Quick, and Delicious Pressure Cooker XL Instant Pot Recipes for Two

By Harold H. Smith

Table of Contents

Introduction

Although it has mainly gained its popularity as the ultimate crowd pleaser, that doesn't mean that the Instant Pot should only be a part of the kitchens of the large households.

This revolutionary appliance can also perfectly satisfy the needs of only two hungry bellies, and this book will definitely convince you in that.

From why you should choose to cook your meals in the Instant Pot to teaching your how to prepare 205 delicious meals to perfection, this cookbook is the ultimate bible for those who know that the love passes through the stomach.

Surprise your loved one with some irresistible delights that are so easy to make that even the busiest workers can master in no time.

Jump to the first recipe and see what I am talking about. Your significant other will be surely pleased.

Instant Pot – The Gem of the Pressure Cookers

If you haven't bought it already, waste no time because the Instant Pot is the single appliance that your kitchen shouldn't be without. And when I say single, I really mean it. Be a proud owner of an Instant Pot and your stovetop and oven will be barely used. Why? Because this amazing kitchen tool is actually a 7-in-1 appliance:

1. It can be used as a pressure cooker
2. You can use it instead of your stove or saute pan.
3. As a rice cooker
4. The IP is also a slow cooker
5. It can be your best warming pot
6. An incredible yogurt maker
7. A hassle-free steamer

The Instant Pot is the true gem in the pressure cooking world. It offers multiple benefits, such as:

- Nutrient Preserving
- Time Saving
- Money Saving
- No Harmful Substances

But, besides these incredible benefits, the thing that makes the IP a king of all the pressure cookers is the fact that it is super functional and specially designed to make pressure cooking a convenient and easy journey.

Its anatomy consists of quite a few buttons, each of them allowing you to cook ready meals with a single click. In short, here is what the IP buttons mean:

Manual Button. This is the most commonly used button, and it allows you to set your own cooking time and pressure, manually.

'+' and '-' Buttons. Increase or decrease the cooking time.

Adjust Button. A click of this button resets the IP's settings to default.

Pressure Button. Switch between high and low pressure.

Keep Warm/Cancel. Keep your meal warm or cancel the cooking.

Steam Button. Steam cook veggies, seafood, and other similar ingredients.

Yogurt Button. This button makes yogurt and pasteurizes milk.

Slow Cook Button. This button allows you to slow cook with the Instant Pot.

Rice Button. Cooks rice and risotto to perfection.

Meat/Stew Button. Helps you cook red meat and stews conveniently.

Poultry Button. Cook chicken and turkey with this button.

Soup Button. The best way to cook your soups in the IP.

Bean/Chili. Perfect for meals with beans.

Multigrain Button. It has never been easier to cook grains.

Porridge Button. Cook your morning porridges with this button.

THE PRESSURE

If the pressure scares you, do not worry. This electric pressure cooker is absolutely safe and durable, and it has no resembles whatsoever to those 1950s pressure cookers that you could explode chickens in.

The pressure can be safely released in two methods:

1. *The Quick Release Method* – You can use this for anything, just remember that if you are cooking food with larger volume or a higher liquid content, your lunch may end up on your kitchen tiles.

2. *The Natural Release Method* – You may be in a hurry to serve your meals but choose this for foamy and higher-in-volume foods and avoid spillage.

THE COOKING TIME

Although, obviously, the cooking time depends on the volume of food you are cooking, whether the food is fresh or frozen, as well as some other factors, however, there is a certain cheat list that every Instant Pot owner should be aware of.

Type of Food	Cooking Time
Beef Roast	35-40 min
Pork Roast	50 min
Beef or Pork Ribs	25 min
Pork and Lamb Chops	5-6 min
Whole Chicken	About 6 min per every lb
Chicken Breasts	8 min
Chicken Thighs	9 min
Fish Fillets	2-3 min
Hard-Boiled Eggs	4 min
Steel-Cut Oats	10 min
Pasta	5 min
White Rice	12 min
Brown Rice	25 min
Dry Beans	25-27 min
Whole Potatoes	12-15 mi
Vegetable Chunks	1-3 min

Obviously, these are just approximate cooking times, and this timetable is not set in stone. The best way to learn is through trial and error, and with the next 205 recipes, you will have numerous chances to learn how long does it take for your IP to cook your favorite food type to your liking.

Just remember to always increase the cooking time by a couple of minutes if using frozen foods, and you're good to go.

Now, let's head to the kitchen, dump some ingredients in your IP and cook tasty meals almost effortlessly.

Breakfast Recipes

1. Apple Breakfast Quinoa

(Total Time: 10 MIN| Serves: 2)

Ingredients:

- 1 Apple, seeded and chopped
- 1 cup Quinoa
- 2 tbsp Cinnamon
- ¼ tsp Salt
- ½ tsp Vanilla Extract
- 1 ½ cups Water

Directions:

1. Pour the water into your IP.
2. Add the remaining ingredients and give it a good stir to combine.
3. Close the lid and set your Instant Pot to MANUAL.
4. Cook for 8 minutes on HIGH.
5. Let the pressure drop on its own.
6. Divide the granola between 2 serving bowls.
7. Serve and enjoy!

(Calories 380| Total Fats 5.5g | Carbs: 7g | Protein 6g |

Fiber 12g)

2. Cheddar Hash Browns

(Total Time: 10 MIN| Serves: 2)

Ingredients:

- ½ cup Frozen Hash Browns
- 2 Eggs
- ¼ cup grated Cheddar Cheese
- 1 ½ Bacon Slices, chopped
- Pinch of Pepper
- ¼ tsp Salt
- 2 tbsp Milk
  1 ½ cups Water

Directions:

1. Add the bacon in your IP and cook in until crispy on SAUTE.
2. Add the hash browns and saute for 2 more minutes.
3. Transfer the mixture to a greased baking dish that can fit into the Instant Pot.
4. Pour the water into your IP and lower the trivet.
5. In a bowl, whisk together the eggs, milk, cheese, salt, and pepper.
6. Pour the mixture over the hash browns.
7. Place the baking dish on the trivet and close the lid.
8. Cook for 5 minutes on MANUAL.
9. Release the pressure quickly. Serve and enjoy!

(Calories 164| Total Fats 11g | Carbs: 7g | Protein 12g |

Fiber 1.5g)

3. Cinnamon Swirl Toast

(Total Time: 35 MIN| Serves: 2)

Ingredients:

- 2 Eggs
- ½ cup Milk
- 1 ½ cups cubes Cinnamon Swirl Bread
- 1 ½ tbsp Maple Syrup
- 1 tsp Butter
- ½ tsp Vanilla
- Pinch of Salt
  1 ½ cups Water

Directions:

1. Pour the water into your IP and lower the trivet.
2. Grease a small baking dish with the butter.
3. Whisk the eggs in a bowl.
4. Whisk in the milk, vanilla, maple, and salt.
5. Arrange the bread cubes in the baking dish and pour the egg mixture over.
6. Place the dish on the trivet and close the lid.
7. Set the IP to MANUAL. Cook on HIGH for 15 minutes.
8. Do a quick pressure release.
9. Serve and enjoy!

(Calories 183| Total Fats 3g | Carbs: 21g | Protein 8g | Fiber 2g)

4. Arugula Eggs with Hollandaise Sauce

(Total Time: 12 MIN| Serves: 2)

Ingredients:

- ¼ cup Arugula
- 2 Mozzarella Slices
- 2 Slices of Whole Wheat Bread, chopped
- 1 ounces Hollandaise Sauce
- 2 Large Eggs
  1 ½ cups Water

Directions:

1. Pour the water into your IP and lower the trivet.
2. Arrange the bread at the bottom of two large (previously greased) ramekins.
3. Chop the arugula and whisk it with the eggs.
4. Divide the egg mixture between the ramekins.
5. Cover the ramekins with aluminum foil and place on the trivet.
6. Close the lid and cook on HIGH for 5 minutes.
7. Do a quick pressure release and discard the foil.
8. Top the eggs with mozzarella and drizzle the sauce over.
9. Serve and enjoy!

(Calories 230| Total Fats 14.6g | Carbs: 9g | Protein 15g | Fiber 0.1g)

5. Banana and Walnut Oatmeal

(Total Time: MIN| Serves: 2)

Ingredients:

- 1 cup Oatmeal
- 1 Cup chopped Walnuts
- 1 Banana, mashed
- 1 2/3 cup Water
- 2 ½ tbsp Honey
- Pinch of Salt

Directions:

1. Pour the water into your IP.
2. Whisk in the honey and banana.
3. Stir in the rest of the ingredients and close the lid.
4. Set the IP to PORRIDGE and cook for 10 minutes.
5. Do a natural pressure release, about 10 minutes.
6. Serve and enjoy!

(Calories 370| Total Fats 12g | Carbs: 50g | Protein 10g |

Fiber 3,4g)

6. Cranberry Bread Pudding

(Total Time: 35 MIN| Serves: 2)

Ingredients:

- 1 cups cubed Cinnamon Raisin Bread
- 2/3 cup Milk
- 1 Egg Yolk
- ¼ cup Sugar
- 2/3 tsp Vanilla Extract
- 1/3 cup dried Cranberries
- Pinch of Salt
  1 ½ cups Warm Water

Directions:

1. Pour the water into your IP and lower the trivet.
2. Whisk together the eggs, sugar, vanilla, salt, and milk, in a bowl.
3. Add the bread in it and let the mixture soak for 15 minutes.
4. Transfer the mixture to a baking dish and cover with aluminum foil.
5. Place the dish on the trivet and close the lid.
6. Cook on HIGH for 12 minutes.
7. Serve and enjoy!

(Calories 313| Total Fats 25g | Carbs: 17g | Protein 11g |

Fiber 21g)

7. Bacon and Egg Sandwich

(Total Time: 20 MIN| Serves: 2)

Ingredients:

- 4 Bread Slices
- 2 Eggs
- 2 tbsp grated Cheese
- 1 tsp Olive Oil
- 4 Bacon Slices
  1 ½ cups Water

Directions:

1. Cook the bacon in the IP on SAUTE until crispy.
2. Crumble it in a bowl.
3. Pour the water into your IP and lower the trivet. Stir in the oil.
4. Divide the bacon between 2 ramekins and crack the eggs over.
5. Sprinkle the cheese on top.
6. Cover the ramekins with foil and place on the trivet.
7. Close the lid and cook on HIGH for 6 minutes.
8. Do a quick pressure release.
9. Assemble the sandwiches and serve.
10. Serve and enjoy!

(Calories 370| Total Fats 13g | Carbs: 31g | Protein 20g |

Fiber 1.5g)

8. Cheesy Mushroom Oats

(Total Time: 30 MIN| Serves: 2)

Ingredients:

- 1 tbsp Butter
- 6 ounces sliced Mushrooms
- ¼ Onion, diced
- ½ cup Steel-Cut Oats
- 1 Thyme Sprig
- 1 tsp minced Garlic
- ¼ cup grated Cheddar Cheese
- 7 ounces Chicken Broth
- ½ cups Water

Directions:

1. Melt the butter in the IP on SAUTE.
2. Add the onions and mushrooms and cook for 3-4 minutes.
3. Add the garlic and cook for one more minute.
4. Place the oats inside and cook for an additional minute.
5. Pour the water and broth over and give it a good stir.
6. Place the thyme sprig inside and close the lid.
7. Cook on HIGH for 12 minutes.
8. Do a natural pressure release. Serve and enjoy!

(Calories 266| Total Fats 12g | Carbs: 31g | Protein 9g |

Fiber 3g)

9. Maple and Vanilla Quinoa Bowl

(Total Time: 20 MIN| Serves: 2)

Ingredients:

- 1 cup Quinoa, uncooked
- 2 tbsp Maple Syrup
- 1 tsp Vanilla Extract
- 2 tbsp Coconut Flakes
  1 ½ cups Water

Directions:

1. Dump all of the ingredients in your Instant Pot.
2. Stir well to combine.
3. Close and seal the lid and set the IP to MANUAL.
4. Cook the mixture for 5-8 minutes on HIGH.
5. Let the pressure come down on its own.
6. Serve and enjoy!

(Calories 372| Total Fats 2.5g | Carbs: 35.7g | Protein 6g | Fiber 3g)

10. Onion, Tomato, and Sweet Potato Frittata

(Total Time: 15 MIN| Serves: 2)

Ingredients:

- 3 Large Eggs, beaten
- 1 tbsp Olive Oil
- 1 tbsp Coconut Flour
- ½ Onion, diced
- 1 Tomato, chopped
- 4 ounces Sweet Potato, shredded
- 2 tbsp Milk
  1 ½ cups Water

Directions:

1. Pour the water into your IP and lower the trivet.
2. Whisk the oil, eggs, and milk in one large bowl.
3. Fold in the flour and veggies.
4. Pour the mixture into a greased baking dish.
5. Place the dish on the trivet and close the lid of the IP.
6. Set the Instant Pot to MANUAL and cook on HIGH for 16 minutes.
7. Do a quick pressure release.
8. Serve and enjoy!

(Calories 202| Total Fats 11.6g | Carbs: 14g | Protein 11g | Fiber 2g)

11. Meat-Loaded Quiche

(Total Time: 40 MIN| Serves: 2)

Ingredients:

- 2 Ham Slices, diced
- ½ cup cooked and crumbled Sausage
- 2 Bacon Slices, cooked and crumbled
- ½ cup grated Cheddar Cheese
- 3 Eggs, beaten
- ¼ cup Milk
- 1 Green Onion, sliced
- Salt and Pepper, to taste
- 1 ½ cups Water

Directions:

1. Pour the water into your IP and lower the trivet.
2. Combine all of the ingredients in a bowl.
3. Pour the mixture into a baking dish.
4. Cover the dish with aluminum foil and place on the trivet.
5. Close the lid and cook on HIGH for 22 minutes.
6. Press CANCEL and wait 10 minutes before releasing the pressure quickly.
7. Serve and enjoy!

(Calories 660| Total Fats 40g | Carbs: 8g | Protein 40g |

Fiber 0.3g)

12. Honey Oatmeal

(Total Time: 10 MIN| Serves: 2)

Ingredients:

- ½ cup Steel-Cut Oats
- ½ cup warm Milk
- 3 tbsp Honey
- Pinch of Cinnamon
- Pinch of Salt
- 2 cups Water

Directions:

1. Pour 1 cup of the water into the Instant Pot and lower the trivet.
2. In a heatproof bowl, place the oats and the remaining water.
3. Close the lid and cook on HIGH for 6 minutes.
4. Do a quick pressure release.
5. Stir in the honey, cinnamon, salt, and milk.
6. Serve and enjoy!

(Calories 155| Total Fats 2g | Carbs: 28g | Protein 4g|

Fiber 2.3g)

13.Egg and Rice Porridge

(Total Time: 40 MIN| Serves: 2)

Ingredients:

- ¼ cup Rice
- 2 Eggs
- 1 cup Water
- 1 cup Chicken Broth
- 2 Scallions, chopped
- ½ tbsp Sugar
- 1 tbsp Olive Oil
- 1 tsp Soy Sauce
- ¼ tsp Salt
- ¼ tsp Pepper

Directions:

1. Combine the rice, water, broth, salt, and sugar, in the Instant Pot.
2. Close the lid and set the IP to PORRIDGE.
3. Cook for 30 minutes.
4. Do a quick pressure release and transfer to a bowl.
5. Wipe the IP clean and add the olive oil.
6. Cook the scallions on SAUTE for about a minute.
7. Add the remaining ingredients and cook until the eggs are set.
8. Stir the mixture into the rice. Serve and enjoy!

(Calories 214| Total Fats 2g | Carbs: 24g | Protein 10g|

Fiber 2.3g)

14. Tomato, Pepper, and Sausage Breakfast

(Total Time: 40 MIN| Serves: 2)

Ingredients:

- 2 Green Bell Peppers, chopped
- 4 Italian Sausage Links
- 14 ounces diced Tomatoes
- 1 Garlic Clove, minced
- 1 tsp Italian Seasoning
- 1 ½ cups Water

Directions:

7. Pour the water into the Instant Pot and lower the trivet.
8. Grease a baking dish with some cooking spray and dump all of the ingredients in it.
9. Stir to combine well.
10. Place the dish in the trivet and close the lid.
11. Set the IP to MANUAL and cook on HIGH for 22 minutes.
12. Release the pressure naturally.
13. Serve and enjoy!

(Calories 400| Total Fats 30g | Carbs: 9g | Protein 20g|

Fiber 0.8g)

15.Orange French Toast

(Total Time: 35 MIN| Serves: 2)

Ingredients:

- 2/3 cup Milk
- 1 Egg
- ¼ tsp Vanilla
- 2 tbsp Sugar
- 1/3 Challah Loaf, chopped
- 2 tbsp melted Butter
- Pinch of Salt
- Zest of 1 Orange
- 1 cups Water

Directions:

1. Pour the water into the Instant Pot and lower the trivet.
2. Place the bread at the bottom of a baking dish.
3. Whisk together the remaining ingredients and pour the mixture over the chopped bread.
4. Place the dish on the trivet.
5. Close and seal the lid and set the IP to MANUAL.
6. Cook on HIGH for 25 minutes.
7. Release the pressure quickly. Serve and enjoy!

(Calories 450| Total Fats 16g | Carbs: 63g | Protein 14g|

Fiber 2)

16. Giant Coconut Pancake

(Total Time: 40 MIN| Serves: 2)

Ingredients:

- ½ cup Coconut Flour
- 2 tbsp Honey
- 1 Egg
- ½ tsp Coconut Extract
- ½ cup ground Almonds
- ¼ tsp Baking Soda
- 1 ½ cups Coconut Milk

Directions:

1. Whisk together the wet ingredients in a bowl.
2. Gently whisk in the remaining ingredients.
3. Coat the IP with some cooking spray and pour the mixture into it.
4. Close the lid and set the Instant Pot to MANUAL.
5. Cook on LOW for 35-40 minutes.
6. Serve and enjoy!

(Calories 350| Total Fats 15g | Carbs: 38g | Protein 16g|

Fiber 18g)

17. Kale and Sausage Egg Casserole

(Total Time: 40 MIN| Serves: 2)

Ingredients:

- 1 tbsp Coconut Oil
- ½ Sweet Potato, shredded
- 3 Eggs
- 4 ounces cooked and crumbled Chorizo
- 1/3 cup sliced Leeks
- ½ cup chopped Kale
- ½ tsp minced Garlic
- 1 ½ cups Water

Directions:

1. Melt the coconut oil in the IP on SAUTE.
2. Add the garlic and leeks and cook for 2 minutes.
3. Stir in the kale and saute for another minute.
4. Beat the eggs and pour over the veggies.
5. Stir in the potatoes and chorizo.
6. Transfer the mixture to a baking dish and pour the water into the IP.
7. Lower the trivet and place the dish on it.
8. Close the lid and cook on HIGH for 20 minutes.
9. Do a quick pressure release. Serve and enjoy!

(Calories 425| Total Fats 30g | Carbs: 13g | Protein 24g|

Fiber 1.6g)

18. Oat Porridge with Pomegranates

(Total Time: 5 MIN| Serves: 2)

Ingredients:

- 1 cup Oats
- 2 tbsp Pomegranate Molasses
- ¾ cups Pomegranate Juice
- A pinch of Salt
- 1 1/2 cups Water
- 1 tbsp Honey, optional

Directions:

1. Combine all of the ingredients, except the molasses, in the Instant Pot and close the lid.
   Set the IP to MANUAL and cook on HIGH for 3 minutes.
2. Release the pressure quickly.
3. Stir in the pomegranate molasses and divide between 2 serving bowls.
4. Serve and enjoy!

(Calories 400| Total Fats 6g | Carbs: 50g | Protein 14g|

Fiber 7)

19. **Black Bean Hash Breakfast**

(Total Time: 15 MIN| Serves: 2)

Ingredients:

- 1 cup grated Sweet Potatoes
- ½ cup chopped Onions
- ½ tsp minces Garlic
- 1/3 cup Veggie Broth
- ½ cup canned Black Beans
- 1 tsp Chili Powder
- 1 tbsp Olive Oil
- 2 tbsp chopped Scallions

Directions:

1. Heat the oil in your Instant Pot on SAUTE.
2. Add the onions and cook for about 3 minutes.
3. Stir in the garlic and cook for another minute.
4. Add the remaining ingredients, give it a good stir, and close the lid.
5. Cook on MANUAL on HIGH for 3 minutes.
6. Release the pressure quickly.
7. Serve and enjoy!

(Calories 140| Total Fats 9g | Carbs: 28g | Protein 5g|

Fiber 2g)

20. Apricot Oat Breakfast

(Total Time: 10 MIN| Serves: 2)

Ingredients:

- 1 cup Coconut Milk
- ½ cup Steel-Cut Oats
- 1 Large Apricot, diced
- ½ tsp Vanilla Extract
- 1 tbsp Honey
- 1 1/2 cups Water

Directions:

1. Pour the coconut milk, vanilla, and oats in the Instant Pot.
2. Stir to combine and close the lid.
3. Cook for 3 minutes on HIGH.
4. Do a natural pressure release, about 10 minutes.
5. Serve and enjoy!

(Calories 240| Total Fats 4g | Carbs: 22g | Protein 4.5g|

Fiber 4g)

21. Dark Chocolate & Cherry Oatmeal

(Total Time: 15 MIN| Serves: 2)

Ingredients:

- ½ cup Steel-Cut Oats
- ½ cup frozen and pitted Cherries
- 2 tbsp Dark Chocolate Chips
- 1 tbsp Sugar
- A pinch of Salt
- 1 ¾ cups Water

Directions:

1. Pour the water into the Instant Pot.
2. Stir in the oats, cherries, salt, and sugar.
3. Close the lid and set the IP to POULTRY.
4. Cook for 12 minutes.
5. Do a quick pressure release.
6. Stir in the chocolate chips.
7. Serve and enjoy!

(Calories 283| Total Fats 6g | Carbs: 54g | Protein 5g|

Fiber 5.5g)

22. Breakfast Burrito

(Total Time: 20 MIN| Serves: 2)

Ingredients:

- 2 Burrito Wraps
- ¼ Onion, sliced
- 2 tsp diced Jalapeno
- ¼ cup diced Ham
- ¼ tsp Taco Seasoning
- 2 Eggs
- ½ cup cubed Potatoes
- ¼ tsp Chili Powder
- 1 1/2 cups Water

Directions:

1. Pour the water into the Instant Pot and lower the trivet.
2. Beat the eggs along with the chili powder and taco seasonings.
3. Pour the mixture into a greased baking dish.
4. Stir in the remaining ingredients, except the wraps.
5. Place the dish on the trivet and cook for 13 minutes on HIGH.
6. Release the pressure quickly.
7. Divide the filling between the burrito wraps, and wrap them up.
8. Serve and enjoy!

(Calories 460| Total Fats 11g | Carbs: 35g | Protein 12g|

Fiber 4)

23. Lemon Tapioca Bowl

(Total Time: 15 MIN| Serves: 2)

Ingredients:

- 2 tbsp Lemon Juice
- ½ cups plus 2 tbsp Milk
- ½ tsp Lemon Zest
- 2 tbsp Brown Sugar
- 1/3 cup Tapioca Pearls
- 1 1/2 cups Water

Directions:

1. Pour the water into the Instant Pot and lower the trivet.
2. Whisk together the remaining ingredients in a baking dish.
3. Place the dish on the lowered trivet.
4. Close the lid and set the IP to STEAM.
5. Cook for 10 minutes and then release the pressure quickly.
6. Serve and enjoy!

(Calories 290| Total Fats 9g | Carbs: 22g | Protein 8g|

Fiber 2g)

24. Cinnamon Breakfast Bread

(Total Time: / MIN| Serves: 2)

Ingredients:

- 1/3 cup Flour
- ¼ tbsp Yeast
- 1 tbsp Flaxseed Meal
- ½ tsp Cinnamon
- 1 tbsp Sugar
- 1/3 cup Hot Water
- Pinch of Sea Salt
- 1 1/2 cups Water

Directions:

1. Pour the water into the Instant Pot and lower the trivet.
2. Combine the dry ingredients in a large bowl.
3. Gently whisk in the wet ingredients until a sticky dough is made.
4. Transfer the dough to a clean and lightly floured surface and knead with your hands for a couple of minutes.
5. Transfer to a greased loaf pan and place on the lowered trivet.
6. Close the lid and cook for 20 minutes on HIGH.
7. Do a quick pressure release.
8. Serve and enjoy!

(Calories 380| Total Fats 5g | Carbs: 41g | Protein 4g|

Fiber 2.1g)

25. Green Bean and Turkey Soup

(Total Time: 35 MIN| Serves: 2)

Ingredients:

- 2/3 cup Green Beans
- ½ pounds Turkey Breasts, diced
- 1/3 cup diced Onions
- 1/3 cup diced Carrots
- 1 small Tomato, chopped
- 2 cups Chicken Stock
- 1 tbsp chopped Parsley
- ½ Turnip, chopped
- ¼ tsp Salt

Directions:

1. Place everything except the green beans in the Instant Pot.
2. Close the lid and set the pot to SOUP.
3. Cook for 20 minutes and then release the pressure quickly.
4. Stir in the green beans and cook for additional 30 minutes.
5. Release the pressure quickly. Serve and enjoy!

(Calories 140| Total Fats 1.5g | Carbs: 15g | Protein 7g|

Fiber 3.2g)

26. Squash and Potato Soup

(Total Time: 35 MIN| Serves: 2)

Ingredients:

- 1 ½ cups Bone Broth
- 1 cups cubed Sweet Potatoes
- 1 cup cubed Butternut Squash
- 1 tbsp Coconut Oil
- ½ Onion, chopped
- 1 Garlic Clove, minced
- ½ tsp Tarragon
- 1 tsp Ginger Powder
- ¼ tsp Turmeric Powder
- ½ tsp Curry Powder
- Salt and Pepper, to taste

Directions:

1. Set your IP to SAUTE and melt the coconut oil in it.
2. Add the onions and cook for 3 minutes.
3. Add the garlic and cook for 30-60 seconds.
4. Add the rest of the ingredients and stir well to combine.
5. Close the lid and cook on MANUAL for 10 minutes.
6. Release the pressure naturally, about 15 minutes.
7. Transfer the soup to a blander or get a hand blender instead.
8. Blend the soup until creamy and smooth.
9. Serve and enjoy!

(Calories 252| Total Fats 6g | Carbs: 20g | Protein 7g| Fiber 2.5g)

27. Creamy Potato and Broccoli Soup with Cheddar

(Total Time: 25 MIN| Serves: 2)

Ingredients:

- ½ cup grated Cheddar Cheese
- ½ cup Half and Half
- 1 pounds Yukon Potatoes, cubed
- ½ Broccoli Head, chopped
- 1 tbsp Butter
- 1 Garlic Clove, minced
- 2 cups Vegetable Broth

Directions:

1. Melt the butter in your Instant Pot on SAUTE.
2. Add garlic and cook for one minute.
3. Add the broth, potatoes, and broccoli, and stir to combine.
4. Close the lid and cook on HIGH for 5 minutes.
5. Do a quick pressure release.
6. Stir in the cheese and cream.
7. Blend with a hand blender immediately.
8. Serve and enjoy!

(Calories 515| Total Fats 32g | Carbs: 24g | Protein 22g|

Fiber 2g)

28. Plantain and Red Bean Stew

(Total Time: 70 | Serves: 2)

Ingredients:

- ½ Plantain, chopped
- 1 Carrot, chopped
- ¼ Onion, chopped
- ¼ pounds dry Red Beans
- 1 tbsp Olive Oil
- ½ Tomato, chopped
- Salt and Pepper, to taste
- Water, as needed

Directions:

1. Heat the oil in the Instant Pot on SAUTE.
2. Add the beans and pour water just to cover them.
3. Close the lid and cook for 30 minutes on HIGH.
4. Do a quick pressure release.
5. Stir in the remaining ingredients and cook for 20-25 more minutes on HIGH.
6. Release the pressure naturally.
7. Serve and enjoy!

(Calories 150| Total Fats 3g | Carbs: 16g | Protein 4g| Fiber 4g)

29. Worcestershire Chili

(Total Time: 55 MIN| Serves: 2)

Ingredients:

- ½ pound ground Beef
- 2 Carrots, slice
- ½ tsp Salt
- 1 tbsp Worcestershire Sauce
- ½ Bell Pepper, chopped
- 14 ounces canned diced Tomatoes
- 2 tsp Chili Powder
- ½ tbsp chopped Parsley
- 1/2 Onion, chopped
- ½ tsp Paprika
- ½ tsp Garlic Powder
- 1 tbsp Olive Oil

Directions:

1. Heat the oil in the Instant Pot on SAUTE.
2. Add onions and cook for 3 minutes.
3. Stir in the spices and cook for 30 more seconds.
4. Add the beef and cook until it becomes browned.
5. Stir in the remaining ingredients.
6. Close the lid and set the IP to MEAT/STEW.
7. Cook at the default setting.
8. Do a natural pressure release.
9. Serve and enjoy!

(Calories 308| Total Fats 9g | Carbs: 21g | Protein 37g| Fiber 3.5g)

30. Chicken Soup with Carrots and Potatoes

(Total Time: 30 MIN| Serves: 2)

Ingredients:

- 1 Frozen Chicken Breast
- 1 large Carrot, sliced
- 8 ounces Chicken Stock
- 8 ounces Water
- 2 Potatoes, cubed
- ¼ Onion, diced
- Salt and Pepper, to taste

Directions:

1. Place all of the ingredients in the Instant Pot.
2. Stir to combine and season with some salt and pepper.
3. Close the lid and set the IP to MANUAL.
4. Cook on HIGH for 30 minutes.
5. Press CANCEL and wait for 10 minutes before releasing the pressure quickly.
6. Shred the chicken with two forks and stir to combine.
7. Serve and enjoy!

(Calories 100| Total Fats 8g | Carbs: 7g | Protein 15g| Fiber 1g)

31.Leek and Potato Soup

(Total Time: 45 MIN| Serves: 2)

Ingredients:

- ¾ cup Half and Half
- 2 ½ cups Veggie Broth
- 2 tsp Butter
- 2 Potatoes, diced
- 1 ½ Leeks, sliced
- 1 Bay Leaf
- 1/3 cup dry White Wine
- ½ tsp Salt
- 1 1/2 cups Water

Directions:

1. Melt the butter in your Instant Pot on SAUTE.
2. Add the leeks and cook for 2-3 minutes.
3. Pour the broth, and wine over.
4. Stir in the potatoes, salt, and bay leaf.
5. Close the lid and set the IP to MANUAL.
6. Cook on HIGH for 10 minutes.
7. Do a quick pressure release and stir in the cream.
8. Blend with a hand blender until creamy.
9. Serve and enjoy!

(Calories 198| Total Fats 8g| Carbs: 21g | Protein 7g|

Fiber 1.2g)

32. Chili and Spicy Chicken Curry

(Total Time: 35 MIN| Serves: 2)

Ingredients:

- ½ can Beans, drained
- 1 tsp Chili Powder
- 1 tsp Cumin
- ½ can Corn, drained
- ½ pound Chicken Breasts
- ½ can chopped Tomatoes, undrained
- 1 ½ cups Chicken Broth

Directions:

1. Place everything in your Instant Pot and stir well to combine.
2. Close and seal the lid and set the IP to MANUAL.
3. Cook for 20 minutes on HIGH.
4. Do a natural pressure release. This shouldn't take longer than 10 minutes.
5. Shred the chicken inside the IP with 2 forks. Stir to combine.
6. Serve and enjoy!

(Calories 604| Total Fats 7g | Carbs: 28g | Protein 32g|

Fiber 2g)

33. Rice and Orange Chickpea Stew

(Total Time: 35 MIN| Serves: 2)

Ingredients:

- 5 ounces Sweet Potatoes, diced
- 1 ½ cups Vegetable Broth
- 10 ounces Chickpeas, canned and drained
- 2 ounces Basmati Rice
- 3 ounces Orange Juice
- ½ tsp Cumin
- 1 tbsp Olive Oil
- ½ Onion, sliced
- Salt and Pepper, to taste

Directions:

1. Set your IP to SAUTE and heat thte oil in it.
2. Add the onions and cook for about 8 minutes.
3. Add the rest of the ingredients and give it a good stir to combine.
4. Set the IP to MANUAL and close the lid.
5. Cook on HIGH for 5 minutes.
6. Do a natural pressure release.
7. Serve and enjoy!

(Calories 270| Total Fats 8g | Carbs: 35g | Protein 9g|

Fiber 5.2g)

34. Ham and Pea Soup

(Total Time: 40 MIN| Serves: 2)

Ingredients:

- ½ Onion, diced
- 1/3 pounds Split Peas, dried
- 2 ½ cups Water
- 1 Celery Stalk, diced
- 1/3 pound Ham Chunks
- 1 Carrot, diced
- ½ tsp Thyme

Directions:

1. Place all of the ingredients in your Instant Pot.
2. Stir well to combine.
3. Close the lid and set the IP to MANUAL.
4. Cook for 20 minutes 0 HIGH. If preferred, cook for an additional 10 minutes.
5. Do a natural pressure release.
6. Serve and enjoy!

(Calories 277| Total Fats 4g | Carbs: 39g | Protein 19g|

Fiber 15g)

35. Beef Soup with Potatoes

(Total Time: 25 MIN| Serves: 2)

Ingredients:

- ¼ pounds ground Beef
- 6 ounces Tomato Sauce
- ½ cups Fresh Corn
- 1 1/2 cups Water
- ¼ Onion, chopped
- 1 cup diced Potatoes
- ½ tsp Hot Pepper Sauce
- ¼ tsp Salt

Directions:

1. Coat your IP with some cooking spray and saute the onions on SAUTE for 2-3 minutes.
2. Add the beef and cook until it becomes browned.
3. Add the remaining ingredients and stir to combine.
4. Close the lid and cook for 6 minutes on HIGH.
5. Do a natural pressure naturally.
6. Serve and enjoy!

(Calories 240| Total Fats 9g | Carbs: 27g | Protein 14g|

Fiber 4.2g)

36. Pumpkin and Corn Chicken Chowder

(Total Time: 15 MIN| Serves: 2)

Ingredients:

- ¼ cup Half and Half
- ½ Onion, diced
- 1 Chicken Breast, chopped
- 14 ounces Chicken Broth
- ½ tsp minced Garlic
- 8 ounces Pumpkin Puree
- 1 Potato, cubed
- 1 cup Corn, frozen
- 1 tbsp Butter
- Pinch of Nutmeg
- Pinch of Pepper
- Pinch of Red Pepper Flakes
- Pinch of Salt

Directions:

1. Set your IP to SAUTE and melt the butter in it.
2. Add the onions and cook for a few minutes, until it becomes translucent.
3. Add the garlic and cook for 30 more seconds.
4. Stir in the spices, pumpkin puree, and pour the broth over.
5. Bring the mixture to a boil on SAUTE and then stir in the corn, potatoes, and chicken.

6. Close the lid and cook on HIGH for 5 minutes.
7. Do a quick pressure release.
8. Stir in the cream.
9. Serve and enjoy!

(Calories 314| Total Fats 21g | Carbs: 16g | Protein 14g|

Fiber 5.8g)

37. Lamb Soup

(Total Time: 40 MIN| Serves: 2)

Ingredients:

- ½ pound Lamb, chopped
- ½ Onion, sliced
- 1 Sweet Potato, cubed
- 1 tbsp Cornstarch
- 1 ½ Carrots, chopped
- 1 1/2 cups Vegetable Broth
- 1 tbsp Olive Oil
- ½ tsp Thyme

Directions:

1. Heat the oil in the Instant Pot on SAUTE.
2. Add the lamb and cook until it is browned on all sides.
3. Add onion and cook for 2 minute.
4. Stir in the remaining ingredients and close the lid.
5. Set the IP to MANUAL.
6. Cook on HIGH for 11 minutes.

7. Release the pressure naturally, for about 10 minutes.
8. Stir in the cornstarch and close the lid.
9. Cook on HIGH for an additional minute or two, until thickened. Serve and enjoy!

(Calories 320| Total Fats 11g | Carbs: 28g | Protein 25g|

Fiber 4g)

38. Minestrone Soup with Tortellini

(Total Time: 15 MIN| Serves: 2)

Ingredients:

- 1 Carrot, diced
- ¼ Onion, diced
- 6 ounces Pasta Sauce
- 1 tbsp Olive Oil
- ¼ tsp Sugar
- 5 ounces canned diced Tomatoes
- 4 ounces dried Cheese Tortellini
- 2 cups Veggie Broth
- 1 tsp minced Garlic
- ½ tsp Italian Seasoning
- 1 Celery Stalk, diced
- 1 1/2 cups Water

Directions:

1. Heat the oil in the Instant Pot on SAUTE.

2. Add the onions, celery, and carrots, and cook for 3 minutes.
3. Add the garlic and cook for an additional minute.
4. Add the remaining ingredients and stir well to combine.
5. Seal the lid and cook for 5 minutes on HIGH.
6. Release the pressure quickly.
7. If the tortellini are too al dente for your taste, cook for an additional minute or two.
8. Serve and enjoy!

(Calories 250| Total Fats 9g | Carbs: 35g | Protein 7g|

Fiber 4g)

39. Pork Shoulder Stew

(Total Time: 65 MIN| Serves: 2)

Ingredients:

- 1 ½ Carrots, sliced
- 1 tsp Cumin
- 1/3 pound String Beans
- 1 Celeriac, chopped
- ½ can diced Tomatoes
- 5 ounces Coconut Milk
- 1 Garlic Clove, minced
- 2/3 pound Pork Shoulder, chopped
- ¼ Onion, diced
- 1 cup Broth

Directions:

1. Dump all of the ingredients in your Instant Pot.
2. Stir to combine and close the lid.
3. Set the IP to STEW and cook at the default cooking time.
4. Do a natural pressure release.
5. Serve and enjoy!

(Calories 650| Total Fats 25g | Carbs: 25g | Protein 60g|

Fiber 6.8g)

40. Vegetable Stew with Tarragon

(Total Time: 25 MIN| Serves: 2)

Ingredients:

- 2 Tomatoes, chopped
- 1 tbsp Olive Oil
- ½ Onion, diced
- 1 Garlic Clove, minced
- 1 cup cubed Red Potatoes
- 2 Carrots, chopped
- 1 cup cubed Parsnips
- ½ cup chopped Red Bell Peppers
- ½ cup cubed Beets
- 2 cups Veggie Broth
- 2 tsp chopped Tarragon

Directions:

1. Heat the olive oil in your Instant Pot on SAUTE.
2. Add the onions and cook for 3 minutes.
3. Stir in the remaining vegies and then cook for additional 3 minutes.
4. Pour the broth over and stir to combine.
5. Close the lid and cook on HIGH for 7 minutes.
6. Do a natural pressure release. Serve and enjoy!

(Calories 354| Total Fats 12g | Carbs: 38g | Protein 13g|

Fiber 5g)

41. Fish Stew

(Total Time: 20 MIN| Serves: 2)

Ingredients:

- 1/3 pound Fish Fillets, chopped
- 2 Potatoes, cubed
- 1 Large carrot, sliced
- ¼ Onion, diced
- 1/3 cup frozen Corn
- 1/3 cup Heavy Cream
- 1 Celery Stalk, diced
- 1 cup Fish Stock
- 1 tbsp Butter
- 1 Bay Leaf
- Salt and Pepper, to taste

Directions:

1. Melt the butter in your IP on SAUTE.
2. Add the onions and cook for about 2-3 minutes.
3. Stir in the remaining ingredients.
4. Seal the lid and cook for 4 minutes on HIGH.
5. Do a natural pressure release.
6. Stir in the heavy cream.
7. Discard the bay leaf before serving and enjoy.

(Calories 1770| Total Fats 12g | Carbs: 14g | Protein 24g|

Fiber 2.5g)

42. Lentil Soup

(Total Time: 40 MIN| Serves: 2)

Ingredients:

- ½ cup dry Lentils
- 2 Garlic Cloves, minced
- 1 Carrot, chopped
- ¼ Onion, diced
- 1 Bay Leaf
- 1 tbsp Olive Oil
- 1 Celery Stalk, chopped
- ½ tsp Cumin
- 2 cups Vegetable Broth
- Salt and Pepper, to taste

Directions:

1. Heat the oil in the IP on SAUTE.

2. Add the onions and celery and cook for 3 minutes.
3. Add garlic and saute for 1 more minute.
4. Stir in the rest of the ingredients and close the lid.
5. Set the IP to MANUAL.
6. Cook for 20 minutes on HIGH.
7. Do a natural pressure release.
8. Serve and enjoy!

(Calories 260| Total Fats 16g | Carbs: 35g | Protein 13g|

Fiber 16g)

43. Turkey Chili

(Total Time: 60 MIN| Serves: 2)

Ingredients:

- ½ cup grated Cheddar Cheese
- 1 tbsp Olive Oil
- 1 Bell Pepper, chopped
- 2 Garlic Cloves, minced
- ¼ tsp Oregano
- 2 tbsp Hot Sauce
- ½ Onion, diced
- ½ pound Ground Turkey
- ½ can Beans, drained
- ½ can diced Tomatoes, undrained
- ¾ cup Chicken Broth
- Salt and Pepper, to taste

Directions:

1. Heat the oil in the IP on SAUTE.
2. Add onions and pepper and cook for 2-3 minutes.
3. Add garlic and oregano and cook for one more minute.
4. Add the turkey and cook for 4-5 minutes.
5. Stir in the remaining ingredients and close the lid.
6. Cook on BEANS/CHILI at the default cooking time.
7. Do a natural pressure release.
8. Season with some salt and pepper.
9. Top with the cheese.
10. Serve and enjoy!

(Calories 700| Total Fats 26g | Carbs: 65g | Protein 65g|

Fiber 18g)

44. Turmeric Carrot Soup with Sweet Potatoes

(Total Time: 35 MIN| Serves: 2)

Ingredients:

- 1 Sweet Potato, chopped
- 2 Carrots, chopped
- 1 tsp Turmeric Powder
- ¼ tsp Paprika
- 1 ½ cups Veggie Broth
- 1 Garlic Clove, minced
- ½ Onion, diced
- 1 tbsp Olive Oil
- Salt and Pepper, to taste

Directions:

1. Heat the oil in the IP on SAUTE.
2. Cook the onion and carrots for 3 minutes.
3. Add the garlic and cook for about a minute.
4. Add the rest of the ingredients and stir to combine. Season with some salt and pepper.
5. Close the lid and cook for 20 minutes on HIGH.
6. Do a quick pressure release.
7. Serve and enjoy!

(Calories 99| Total Fats 3g | Carbs: 16g | Protein 4g| Fiber 2g)

45. Brisket and Mushroom Stew

(Total Time: 30 MIN| Serves: 2)

Ingredients:

- ½ Onion, diced
- 2 Red Potatoes, cubed
- 2 Carrots, chopped
- 5 ounces Golden Mushroom Soup
- 6 ounces Water
- 1 tbsp Canola Oil
- 2/3 pound Beef Brisket, chopped
- 4 ounces Button Mushrooms, sliced
- ½ tsp Parsley

Directions:

1. Heat the oil in the IP on SAUTE.
2. Add the meat and cook until browned on all sides.
3. Add the onion and cook for 2 more minutes.
4. Stir in the rest of the ingredients.
5. Close the lid and set the IP to MANUAL.
6. Cook on HIGH for 15 minutes.
7. Let the pressure drop naturally.
8. Serve and enjoy!

(Calories 525| Total Fats 17g | Carbs: 50g | Protein 42g|

Fiber 6g)

46. Navy Bean and Ham Shank Soup

(Total Time: 30 MIN| Serves: 2)

Ingredients:

- ½ cups dried Beans, soaked overnight and rinsed
- 1/2 pound Ham Shank
- ¼ Onion, died
- 1 Carrot, sliced
- 1 Celery Stalk, diced
- 1 Garlic Clove, minced
- ½ cup Tomato Sauce
- 1 tbsp Olive Oil
- ¼ tsp Salt
- ½ Bell Pepper, chopped
- 1 1/2 cups Water

Directions:

1. Set your Instant Pot to SAUTE and heat the oil in it.
2. Add the onions, carrots, pepper, and celery, and cook for 3 minutes.
3. Stir in the garlic and cook for 1 more minute.
4. Add the rest of the ingredients and stir well to combine.
5. Close the lid and set the IP to MANUAL.
6. Cook on HIGH for 20 minutes.
7. Let the pressure drop naturally.
8. Serve and enjoy!

(Calories 640| Total Fats 32g | Carbs: 45g | Protein 35g| Fiber 16g)

47. Lemony Chicken with Currants

(Total Time: 20 MIN| Serves: 2)

Ingredients:

- 1 Lemon, sliced
- 3 tbsp Currants
- 2/3 pound Chicken Fillets
- 1 tbsp Canola Oil
- 1 Garlic Clove, minced
- 1/3 cup chopped Scallions
- 1/3 cup Green Olives
- 1 ¼ cup Water
- Salt and Pepper, to taste

Directions:

1. Heat the oil in the IP on SAUTE.
2. Add the onions, scallions, and garlic, and saute for 3 minutes.
3. Place the chicken inside and arrange the olives and currants over.
4. Top with the lemon slices.
5. Season with some salt and pepper and pour the water over.
6. Cook for 15 minutes on POULTRY.
7. Do a quick pressure release.
8. Serve and enjoy!

(Calories 300| Total Fats 16g | Carbs: 7g | Protein 33g| Fiber 1g)

48. Chicken Casserole with Rice and Artichokes

(Total Time: 25 MIN| Serves: 2)

Ingredients:

- ¼ tsp Garlic Powder
- ¼ Onion, diced
- 1 cup diced canned Tomatoes
- 1 tbsp Olive Oil
- ½ pound Chicken Breast, cubed
- ¼ cup dry White Wine
- 1 cup Chicken Broth
- 1/3 cup Rice
- 4 ounces Artichokes Hearts, chopped

Directions:

1. Heat the olive oil in the IP on SAUTE and add the onions.
2. Cook for 2 minutes and then add the chicken and garlic powder.
3. Cook until golden on all sides.
4. Add the remaining ingredients and stir well to combine.
5. Close the lid and cook for 10 minutes on HIGH.
6. Release the pressure naturally.

7. Serve and enjoy!

(Calories 550| Total Fats 19g | Carbs: 34g | Protein 30g|

Fiber 3g)

49. Sweet Onion and Pear Chicken

(Total Time: 25MIN| Serves: 2)

Ingredients:

- 1 tbsp Butter
- ½ pound Boneless Chicken Thighs, chopped
- 1 Large Pear, sliced
- 1 tbsp Balsamic Vinegar
- ½ cup diced Sweet Onions
- 1 ¼ cup Chicken Stock
- Salt and Pepper, to taste

Directions:

1. Melt the butter in the Instant Pot on SAUTE.
2. Add the onions and cook for 5 minutes.
3. Add the chicken and cook until browned on all sides.
4. Dump the rest of the ingredients and stir to combine.
5. Close the lid and cook on HIGH for 15 minutes.
6. Do a quick pressure release.
7. Serve and enjoy!

(Calories 290| Total Fats 7g | Carbs: 13.5g | Protein 40g|

Fiber 2g)

50. Orange and Cranberry Turkey Wings

(Total Time: 40 MIN| Serves: 2)

Ingredients:

- ½ pound Turkey Wings
- ½ Butter Stick
- 1 ¼ cup Veggie Stock
- 1 Onion, sliced
- ¼ cup Orange Juice
- 1 cup Cranberries
- Salt and Pepper, to taste

Directions:

1. Melt the butter in your IP and brown the wings on all sides. Transfer to a plate.
2. Add the onions and saute for a few minutes.
3. Add the cranberries and orange juice and cook for 5 more minutes.
4. Return the wings to the pot and pour the water over. Season with some salt and pepper and close the lid.
5. Cook for 15 minutes on POULTRY.
6. Do a quick pressure release and set to SAUTE.
7. Cook for 5 more minutes, until the sauce thickens.
8. Serve and enjoy!

(Calories 460| Total Fats 28g | Carbs: 14g | Protein 34g|

Fiber 1.2g)

51.Chicken and Fried Rice

(Total Time: 25 MIN| Serves: 2)

Ingredients:

- 1 tbsp Butter
- 2/3 cup chopped Chicken
- 2 tsp Apple Cider Vinegar
- 2 tbsp chopped Green Onions
- 1 Carrot, chopped
- ½ cup Rice
- Salt and Pepper, to taste
- 1 ¾ cup Chicken Broth

Directions:

1. Place all of the ingredients in your Instant Pot.
2. Stir the ingredients well to combine.
3. Close the lid and cook on RICE for 20 minutes.
4. Do a quick pressure release.
5. Fluff the rice with a fork and stir to combine everything.
6. Serve and enjoy!

(Calories 430| Total Fats 10g | Carbs: 55g | Protein 20g|

Fiber 9g)

52. Bean and Tomato Chicken

(Total Time: 20 MIN| Serves: 2)

Ingredients:

- 1 tbsp Oil
- ½ pound Chicken Breast, chopped
- 5 ounces canned Beans
- 5 ounces canned diced Tomatoes
- 2/3 cup Vegetable Stock
- ¼ cup Sour Cream
- Salt and Pepper, to taste

Directions:

1. Heat the oil in the Instant Pot on SAUTE.
2. Add the chicken and cook until golden.
3. Stir in the remaining ingredients.
4. Close the lid and set the IP to SAUTE.
5. Cook for 10 minutes.
6. Do a quick pressure release.
7. Serve and enjoy!

(Calories 350| Total Fats 8g | Carbs: 22g | Protein 5g|

Fiber 5g)

53. Turkey Risotto with Veggies

(Total Time: 25 MIN| Serves: 2)

Ingredients:

- ¾ cup cooked and shredded Turkey
- 1 tbsp Butter
- 1/3 cup chopped Zucchini
- 1/3 cup chopped Rutabaga
- 1/3 cup chopped Carrots
- ½ cup chopped Swiss Chard
- 1 tsp Soy Sauce
- 2/3 cup Arborio Rice
- 2 ¼ cup Broth

Directions:

1. Place all of the ingredients in the Instant Pot.
2. Stir to combine and set the IP to RICE.
3. Cook for 18 minutes.
4. Do a quick pressure release.
5. Fluff with a fork and stir again to combine.
6. Serve and enjoy!

(Calories 580| Total Fats 20g | Carbs: 51g | Protein 44g|

Fiber 17g)

54. Turkey Sausage Pilaf

(Total Time: 25 MIN| Serves: 2)

Ingredients:

- 1 Turkey Sausage, sliced
- 2/3 cup Rice
- 1 cup Spinach
- 1 Carrot, chopped
- 1 Shallot, chopped
- 1 tsp minced Garlic
- 1 tbsp Olive Oil
- 1 Bell Pepper, diced
- 2 ¼ cups Vegetable Broth
- Salt and Pepper, to taste

Directions:

1. Heat the oil in the Instant Pot on SAUTE.
2. Add the shallots, peppers, and garlic, and cook for 3 minutes.
3. Add rice and cook for 30 seconds.
4. Stir in the rest of the ingredients.
5. Set the IP to BEAN/CHILI and cook for 12 minutes.
6. Do a natural pressure release.
7. Fluff with a fork before serving. Enjoy!

(Calories 350| Total Fats 56g | Carbs: 55g | Protein 17g|

Fiber 15.8g)

55. Grapefruit and Cashew Chicken Fillets

(Total Time: 30 MIN| Serves: 2)

Ingredients:

- 1/2 pound Chicken Fillets
- 1 tsp Cornstarch
- ¼ cup chopped Cashews
- ½ cup Grapefruit Juice
- 1 tbsp Olive Oil
- 2/3 cup Water
- Salt and Pepper, to taste

Directions:

1. Heat the oil in the Instant Pot on SAUTE.
2. Add chicken and cook until no longer pink.
3. Stir in the rest of the ingredients except the cornstarch.
4. Close the lid and cook on POULTRY for 10 minutes.
5. Do a quick pressure release.
6. Whisk in the cornstarch and cook on SAUTE until the mixture thickens.
7. Serve and enjoy!

(Calories 347| Total Fats 16g | Carbs: 14g | Protein 38g|

Fiber 3g)

56. Buffalo Chicken with Potatoes

(Total Time: 35 MIN| Serves: 2)

Ingredients:

- ½ Onion, diced
- 8 ounces Potatoes, diced
- 2 tbsp Buffalo Sauce
- ¼ tsp Garlic Powder
- 1 ½ tbsp Butter
- ½ pound Chicken Breast, chopped
- 2/3 cup Chicken Broth
- ¼ tsp Salt
- Pinch of Pepper

Directions:

1. Melt the butter in your Instant Pot on SAUTE.
2. Add the onions and saute for 3 minutes.
3. Stir in the rest of the ingredients and close the lid.
4. Set the IP to POULTRY.
5. Cook for 15-18 minutes.
6. Do a quick pressure release.
7. Serve and enjoy!

(Calories 290| Total Fats 12g | Carbs: 25g | Protein 20g|

Fiber 1g)

57. Creamy Paprika Goose

(Total Time: 30 MIN| Serves: 2)

Ingredients:

- ½ Onion, diced
- 2/3 pound Goose Breasts, chopped
- 1 Bell Pepper, diced
- 1 ½ tsp Paprika
- ½ cup Coconut Cream
- 1 tbsp Butter
- 1 Garlic Clove, minced
- 8 ounces Tomato Sauce

Directions:

1. Set your Instant Pot to SAUTE and melt the butter in it.
2. Add the onions and pepper and cook for 3-4 minutes.
3. Add the garlic and cook for 30-60 seconds.
4. Place the goose inside and cook until it is no longer pink.
5. Pour the tomato sauce over and stir in the paprika.
6. Close the lid and cook on POULTRY for 12 minutes.
7. Do a natural pressure release.
8. Stir in the coconut cream.
9. Serve and enjoy!

(Calories 496| Total Fats 25g | Carbs: 18g | Protein 48g|

Fiber 2g)

58. Turkey Patties

(Total Time: 30 MIN| Serves: 2)

Ingredients:

- ½ pound Ground Turkey
- ¼ cup Breadcrumbs
- 1 Egg
- 1 ½ cups Chicken Broth
- 1 tbsp Olive Oil
- ¼ tsp Garlic Powder
- ½ tsp dried Parsley
- Salt and Pepper, to taste

Directions:

1. Pour the water into the Instant Pot and lower the trivet.
2. In a bowl, combine the turkey, parsley, egg, spices, and breadcrumbs,
3. Make 4 smaller patties out of the mixture.
4. Arrange on a greased baking dish and place on the trivet.
5. Cook for 5 minutes on HIGH.
6. Do a quick pressure release, and discard the cooking liquid.
7. Wipe the pot clean and heat the oil in it on SAUTE.
8. Add the patties and cook until crispy and golden.
9. Serve and enjoy!

(Calories 255| Total Fats 15g | Carbs: 8.5g | Protein 25g|

Fiber 1g)

59. Chicken Cajun Pasta

(Total Time: 25 MIN| Serves: 2)

Ingredients:

- 8 ounces Bowtie Pasta
- 1 ½ tbsp Cajun Seasoning
- 6 ounces Coconut Cream
- 6 ounces diced Chicken Breasts
- ¼ cup diced Bell Peppers
- ¼ cup diced Red Onions
- 1 ½ tbsp Butter
- 4 ounces Chicken Broth

Directions:

1. Melt the butter in the IP on SAUTE.
2. Add onions and peppers and cook for 3 minutes.
3. Add the chicken and cook for 3 more minutes.
4. Stir in the remaining ingredients.
5. Close the lid and cook on HIGH for 8 minutes.
6. Do a quick pressure release.
7. Serve and enjoy!

(Calories 670| Total Fats 25g | Carbs: 75g | Protein 30g|

Fiber 1.5g)

60. Duck a l'Orange

(Total Time: 50 MIN| Serves: 2)

Ingredients:

- 1 Duck Breast, cut in half
- 1 tbsp Fish Sauce
- 1 Duck Leg, cut in half
- 1 tbsp minced Ginger
- 4 Spring Onions, chopped
- 1 Red Chili, chopped
- 1 tsp chopped Lemongrass
- 1 Whole Star Anise
- 1 ½ cups Orange Juice

Directions:

1. Grease the IP with some cooking spray.
2. Add the duck (skin-side down) and cook until it becomes crispy. Transfer the duck to a plate.
3. Add the ginger and cook for 30 seconds.
4. Add the remaining ingredients and return the duck to the pot.
5. Close the lid and cook for 30 minutes on HIGH.
6. Do a natural pressure release.
7. Serve and enjoy!

(Calories 442| Total Fats 22g | Carbs: 9g | Protein 50g|

Fiber 1g)

61. Pina Colada Chicken

(Total Time: 35 MIN| Serves: 2)

Ingredients:

- 1 tbsp Coconut Aminos
- ¼ cup Coconut Cream
- ¼ cup chopped Green Onion
- Pinch of Cinnamon
- ½ cup Pineapple Chunks
- 2/3 pounds Chicken Thighs, boneless
- ½ cup Water

Directions:

1. Place the chicken, pineapple, coconut aminos, and cinnamon in the IP.
2. Add the coconut cream and stir to combine.
3. Pour the water over and close the lid.
4. Cook on POULTRY for 15 minutes.
5. Do a quick pressure release.
6. Serve topped with green onions.
7. Enjoy!

(Calories 530| Total Fats 2g | Carbs: 11g | Protein 65g|

Fiber 1.5g)

Note: Coconut aminos is usually used as a substitute for soy sauce, people that are gulten-sensitive usually use it. People that consume gluten can substitute it with soy sauce.

62. Ground Chicken and Porcini Risotto

(Total Time: 15 MIN| Serves: 2)

Ingredients:

- 1 cup sliced Porcini Mushrooms
- 1 cup ground Chicken
- 1 cup Basmati Rice
- 1 Shallot, chopped
- 2 cups Chicken Stock
- 1 tbsp Olive Oil
- ¼ cup chopped Celery
- Pinch of Paprika
- Salt and Pepper, to taste

Directions:

1. Heat the oil in the Instant Pot on SAUTE.
2. Add the shallots and celery and cook for 2 minutes.
3. Add the mushrooms and cook for 3 minutes more.
4. Add chicken and cook until it becomes golden.
5. Stir in the remaining ingredients.
6. Close the lid and set the instant pot to RICE.
7. Cook for 8 minutes.
8. Do a natural pressure release.
9. Serve and enjoy!

(Calories 610| Total Fats 11g | Carbs: 88g | Protein 32g|

Fiber 14g)

63. Peach Chicken Bake

(Total Time: 25 MIN| Serves: 2)

Ingredients:

- ½ chopped canned Peaches in Syrup
- ½ pound Chicken Fillets
- 1 tbsp Oyster Sauce
- 1 tsp Sugar
- ½ tsp Onion Powder
- ¼ tsp Cayenne Pepper
- ½ cup Water

Directions:

1. Grease the Instant Pot with cooking spray.
2. Add the chicken and cook until golden.
3. Sprinkle with cayenne, onion powder, and sugar.
4. Add the oyster sauce, and peaches and stir to combine well.
5. Pour the water over and close the lid.
6. Select MEAT/STEW and cook for 10 minutes.
7. Do a quick pressure release.
8. Serve and enjoy!

(Calories 480| Total Fats 16g | Carbs: 15g | Protein 32g|

Fiber 1g)

64. Sweet and Sour Chicken with Mangos

(Total Time: 35 MIN| Serves: 2)

Ingredients:

- 4 smallish Chicken Thighs
- 1 Garlic Clove, minced
- 1 tsp minced Ginger
- 1 Mango, chopped
- 2 tbsp Lime Juice
- 1 tsp Fish Sauce
- 2 tbsp Coconut Aminos
- 2 tbsp chopped Cilantro
- 1 tbsp Honey
- 1 tbsp Apple Cider Vinegar
- 1 tbsp Olive Oil
- 2/3 cup Chicken Broth

Directions:

1. Heat the oil in the IP on SAUTE and cook the chicken thighs until golden on both sides. Transfer to a plate.
2. Add the onions, garlic, ginger, and mango, and cook for 2 minutes.
3. Stir in the remaining ingredients and return the chicken to the pot.
4. Close the lid and set the IP to POULTRY.
5. Cook for 12 minutes.
6. Do a quick pressure release.

7. If desired, cook for a few more minutes on SAUTE for a thicker sauce.
8. Serve and enjoy!

(Calories 380| Total Fats 13g | Carbs: 26g | Protein 27g|

Fiber 4g)

65. Turkey Casserole

(Total Time: MIN| Serves: 2)

Ingredients:

- 2 Turkey Breasts
- 1 Celery Stalk, chopped
- 1 can Cream of Mushroom Soup
- ½ cup Chicken Broth
- ½ bag of Pepperidge Stuffing Cubes
- ½ Onion, chopped

Directions:

1. Place everything inside your Instant Pot.
2. Stir well to combine and close the lid.
3. Set the Instant Pot to MANUAL and cook on HIGH for 25 minutes.
4. Let the pressure drop naturally.
5. Serve and enjoy!

(Calories 650| Total Fats 20g | Carbs: 60g | Protein 45g | Fiber 2g)

66. Apple and Raisin Goose

(Total Time: 25 MIN| Serves: 2)

Ingredients:

- ½ Shallot, chopped
- ½ tsp Dill
- 2/3 pound Goose Breasts, chopped
- 1 Apple, sliced
- 1 tbsp Butter
- ¼ cup Rasisins
- 2/3 cup Chicken Broth

Directions:

1. Melt the butter in the IP on SAUTE.
2. Add the goose and cook until it is no longer pink.
3. Add the rest of the ingredients to the Instant Pot.
4. Stir well to incorporate them well.
5. Close the lid and set the IP to MANUAL.
6. Cook for 15 minutes on HIGH.
7. Do a quick pressure release.
8. Serve and enjoy!

(Calories 260| Total Fats 10g | Carbs: 14g | Protein 30g|

Fiber 2,1g)

67. Chicken Verde Brown Rice Casserole

(Total Time: 35 MIN| Serves: 2)

Ingredients:

- 1/3 cup Salsa Verde
- 2/3 pound Chicken Breasts
- ½ Onion, sliced
- ½ cup Brown Rice
- 2/3 cup Chicken Broth

Directions:

1. Combine everything in your Instant Pot.
2. Close and seal the lid and set it to MANUAL.
3. Cook on HIGH for 8 minutes.
4. Do a natural pressure release,
5. Transfer the chicken to a cutting board and shred with two forks.
6. Return to the pot and give it a good stir.
7. Serve and enjoy!

(Calories 420| Total Fats 5g | Carbs: 45g | Protein 45g|

Fiber 7.4g)

68. Alfredo Chicken Fettucine

(Total Time: 10MIN| Serves: 2)

Ingredients:

- ¾ cup cooked and shredded Chicken Meat
- 8 ounces Alfredo Sauce
- 7 ounces Fettucine
- 2 cups Water
- ¼ tsp Garlic Powder
- ¼ tsp Salt
- Pinch of Pepper

Directions:

1. Place everything in the Instant Pot.
2. Give it a good stir to combine.
3. Set the IP to MANUAL.
4. Cook on HIGH for 4 minutes.
5. Do a quick pressure release.
6. Serve topped with some shredded cheese, if desired.
7. Enjoy!

(Calories 490| Total Fats 16g | Carbs: 60g | Protein 27g|

Fiber 3.5g)

69. Chicken Spaghetti with Spinach in a Mushroom Sauce

(Total Time: 20 MIN| Serves: 2)

Ingredients:

- 2 cups Broth
- 2 ounces shredded Mozzarella Cheese
- 1 Chicken Breast, chopped
- 1 can Creamy Mushroom Soup
- 1 Garlic Clove, minced
- 2 cups Baby Spinach
- 8 ounces Spaghetti

Directions

1. Set your Instant Pot to SAUTE.
2. Combine the chicken and broth inside.
3. Bring the mixture to a boil.
4. Stir in the remaining ingredients, close the lid, and set the Instant Pot to MANUAL.
5. Cook on HIGH for 4 minutes.
6. Do a quick pressure release.
7. Serve and enjoy!

(Calories 520| Total Fats 12g | Carbs: 60g | Protein 27g|

Fiber 3g)

70. Apricot Glazed Halved Turkey

(Total Time: 60 MIN| Serves: 2)

Ingredients:

- ½ Small Turkey
- 2 ounces Apricot Jam
- 1 Carrot, diced
- ¼ Onion, diced
- 1 ¼ cup Chicken Stock
- ¼ tsp Cumin
- ¼ tsp Coriander
- ¼ tsp Salt

Directions:

1. In a small bowl, combine the apricot jam and all of the spices.
2. Rub the glaze over the turkey.
3. Place the turkey inside the Instant Pot.
4. Add the carrot and onion.
5. Pour the broth around (not over) the turkey.
6. Close the lid and set the IP to POULTRY.
7. Cook for 25 minutes.
8. Do a natural pressure release.
9. Serve and enjoy!

(Calories 880| Total Fats 20g | Carbs: 80g | Protein 100 g| Fiber 5g)

71.Mongolian Beef

(Total Time: 25 MIN| Serves: 2)

Ingredients:

- 2/3 pound Flank Steak
- 1 Carrot, shredded
- ½ tsp minced Garlic
- 1/3 cup Soy Sauce
- ½ tsp minced Ginger
- ¼ cup Brown Sugar
- 1 tbsp Olive Oil
- 5 tbsp Water
- 2 tbsp Cornstarch

Directions:

1. Slice the beef into strips.
2. In the IP, combine the soy sauce, ginger, sugar, garlic, oil, and half of the water.
3. Stir in the flank slices and carrot.
4. Close the lid and set to IP to MANUAL.
5. Cook on HIGH for 7 minutes.
6. Release the pressure naturally.
7. Whisk together the remaining water and cornstarch and stir into the sauce.
8. Cook on SAUTE until thickened.
9. Serve and enjoy!

(Calories 480| Total Fats 17g | Carbs: 29g | Protein 51g|

Fiber 1g)

72. Instant Beef and Noodles

(Total Time: 60 MIN| Serves: 2)

Ingredients:

- ½ pound Boneless Chuck
- 1 tbsp Oil
- 8 ounces Noodles
- 1 Garlic Clove, minced
- ¼ Onion, chopped
- 1 cup Water

Directions:

1. Cut the beef into cubes.
2. Heat the oil in the IP and add the onion and garlic.
3. Cook for 2 minutes.
4. Add beef and cook until browned on all sides.
5. Pour the water over and cook on MANUAL for 25 minutes.
6. Do a quick pressure release.
7. Add the noodles and cook for 4 more minutes.
8. Release the pressure quickly.
9. Serve and enjoy!

(Calories 620| Total Fats 27g | Carbs: 26g | Protein 54g|

Fiber 1g)

73. Pork Ribs with Sauerkraut

(Total Time: 40 MIN| Serves: 2)

Ingredients:

- ½ pound Pork Ribs
- 5 ounces Kielbasa, sliced
- 1 tsp Brown Sugar
- 1 tbsp Olive Oil
- 10 ounces Sauerkraut
- ¼ tsp Pepper
- 1/3 cup Water

Directions:

1. Heat the oil in the IP and add the pork ribs.
2. Cook until browned on both sides.
3. Add the remaining ingredients and stir well to combine.
4. Close the lid and set the IP to MANUAL.
5. Cook for 15 minutes on HIGH.
6. Do a natural pressure release.
7. Serve and enjoy!

(Calories 400| Total Fats 27g | Carbs: 9g | Protein 28g|

Fiber 0g)

74. Beef Taco Pie with Cheese

(Total Time: 20 MIN| Serves: 2)

Ingredients:

- ½ pound Ground Beef
- 6 ounces Mexican Cheese Blend
- ½ packet Taco Seasoning
- 3 Tortillas
- 1/4 cup Refried Beans
- 1 cup Water

Directions:

1. Pour the water into the IP ad lower the trivet.
2. In a greased baking dish, place one tortilla.
3. Combine the remaining ingredients in a bowl.
4. Place ½ of the mixture on top of the tortilla.
5. Place another tortilla on top and arrange the remaining filling.
6. Top with the third tortilla.
7. Place the dish in the IP and close the lid.
8. Cook on MNAUAL for 12 minutes.
9. Do a quick pressure release.
10. Serve and enjoy!

(Calories 360| Total Fats 19g | Carbs: 29g | Protein 25g|

Fiber 6g)

75. Beef Brisket with Veggies

(Total Time: 70 MIN | Serves: 2)

Ingredients:

- 2/3 pound Beef Brisket
- 3 Red Potatoes, chopped
- 2 tbsp Olive Oil
- 1 cup chopped Carrots
- 1 Garlic Clove, minced
- ½ Onion, chopped
- 1 Celery Stalk, chopped
- 1 Bay Leaf
- 1 ½ tbsp Worcestershire Sauce
- 1 cup Beef Broth

Directions:

1. Heat half of the oil in the IP and add the beef.
2. Sear on all sides and then transfer to a plate.
3. Heat the remaining oil and add the onions and celery.
4. Cook for 2 minutes and then add the garlic.
5. Cook for another minute.
6. Stir in the veggies and pour the broth over.
7. Top with the beef, add the bay leaf and drizzle the Worcestershire sauce over.
8. Close the lid and cook for 45 minutes on MANUAL.
9. Serve and enjoy!

(Calories 400| Total Fats 18g | Carbs: 10g | Protein 28g|

Fiber 1g)

76. BBQ Baby Back Ribs

(Total Time: 55 MIN| Serves: 2)

Ingredients:

- 1 ½ pounds Baby Back Ribs
- 1 cup Beer
- 6 ounces Barbecue Sauce
- 2 tsp Olive Oil
- ¼ tsp Onion Powder
- ¼ tsp Pepper
- ¼ tsp Garlic Salt
- ¼ tsp Paprika

Directions:

1. Cut the baby ribs into pieces.
2. Combine the spices in a small bowl and rub into the meat.
3. Heat the oil in the IP on SAUTE and brown the meat on all sides.
4. Pour the beer over and close the lid.
5. Cook on HIGH for 25 minutes.
6. Do a quick pressure release.
7. Discard the liquid and brush the ribs with BBQ sauce.
8. Cook on SAUTE until sticky. Serve and enjoy!

(Calories 230| Total Fats 7g | Carbs: 36g | Protein 8g|

Fiber 0.5g)

77. Pork Roast with Cinnamon and Cranberries

(Total Time: 75 MIN| Serves: 2)

Ingredients:

- 1 tbsp Apple Cider Vinegar
- 2/3 pound Pork Roast
- 6 ounces Fresh Cranberries
- 1 tbsp chopped Herbs
- 10 ounces Beef Broth
- 1 tbsp Honey
- 1 tbsp Butter
- ¼ tsp Garlic Powder
- ¼ tsp Cinnamon

Directions:

1. Melt the butter in the Instant Pot on SAUTE.
2. Add the pork and sear on all sides.
3. Add the rest of the ingredients and stir well to combine.
4. Close the lid and set the IP to MANUAL.
5. Cook for 55 minutes on HIGH.
6. Do a natural pressure release. Serve and enjoy!

(Calories 680| Total Fats 38g | Carbs: 30g | Protein 45g|

Fiber 1.5g)

78. Rosemary-Flavored Lamb with Carrots

(Total Time: 35 MIN| Serves: 2)

Ingredients:

- ¾ pound Boneless Lamb, chopped
- 1 tbsp Flour
- ½ cup sliced Carrots
- 2 Rosemary Spigs
- 1 tbsp Olive Oil
- 1 ½ cup Beef Stock
- 1 ½ tsp minced Garlic
- Salt and Pepper, to taste

Directions:

1. Season the lamb with some salt and pepper.
2. Heat the oil in the IP on SAUTE.
3. Add the lamb and sear on all sides.
4. Whisk together the flour and stock and pour over the lamb.
5. Add the remaining ingredients and close the lid.
6. Cook on HIGH for 20 minutes.
7. Do a quick pressure release.
8. Serve and enjoy!

(Calories 290| Total Fats 2g | Carbs: 14.3g | Protein 40g| Fiber 3g)

79. Honey and Mustard Pork Chops

(Total Time: 20 MIN| Serves: 2)

Ingredients:

- 1 pound Pork Chops
- ½ tbsp Maple Syrup
- 2 tbsp Honey
- 1 ½ tbsp Dijon Mustard
- ½ tsp grated Ginger
- ¼ tsp Cinnamon
- Pinch of Pepper
- ¼ tsp Salt
- 2/3 cup Beef Broth

Directions:

1. Grease the IP with cooking spray and place the pork chops inside.
2. Cook until browned on all sides.
3. In a bowl, whisk together the remaining ingredients.
4. Pour the mixture over the pork.
5. Closet the lid and cook on HIGH for 15 minutes.
6. Do a quick pressure release.
7. Serve and enjoy!

(Calories 800| Total Fats 55g | Carbs: 20g | Protein 50g|

Fiber 1g)

80. Round Steak with Veggies

(Total Time: 40 MIN| Serves: 2)

Ingredients:

- ½ pound Round Steak, cubed
- 1 tbsp Butter
- 1 Carrot, sliced
- 2 Bell Peppers, chopped
- ½ cup of Mushroom Slices
- 2 Potatoes, cubed
- ½ tsp Garlic Salt
- 1 ½ cup Beef Broth
- 1 tbsp Flour
- ¼ tsp Onion Powder

Directions:

1. Toss the steak cubes with flour.
2. Melt the butter in the IP on SAUTE.
3. Add the steak and cook until browned on all sides.
4. Stir in the remaining ingredients and close the lid.
5. Cook on MEAT/STEW for about half an hour.
6. Serve and enjoy!

(Calories 306| Total Fats 9g | Carbs: 21g | Protein 35g|

Fiber 1g)

81. Beef Bourguignon

(Total Time: 75 MIN| Serves: 2)

Ingredients:

- ½ cup Red Wine
- 1 cup Beef Broth
- 1 Sweet Potato, cubed
- 1 Garlic Clove, minced
- ½ Onion, chopped
- ½ pound Beef, cubed
- 1 tbsp Olive Oil
- 2 Carrots, chopped
- 1 tbsp Maple Syrup
- ¼ pound Bacon Tips

Directions:

1. Heat the oil in the IP and add the onion.
2. Cook for 3 minutes.
3. Add the garlic and saute for 1 minute.
4. Add the beef and cook until it becomes browned on all sides.
5. Stir in the bacon and cook for an additional minute.
6. Add the rest of the ingredients and stir the mixture well to combine.
7. Close the lid and set the IP to MANUAL.
8. Cook on HIGH for 30 minutes.
9. Do a natural pressure release.
10. Serve and enjoy!

(Calories 700| Total Fats 34g | Carbs: 30g | Protein 57g| Fiber 2g)

82. Pepperoncini Pot Roast

(Total Time: 55 MIN| Serves: 2)

Ingredients:

- 2/3 pound Beef Roast
- 2 tbsp Butter
- 1 packet Gravy Mix
- ½ cup Pepperoncini Juice
- 2 Pepperoncini, chopped
- ½ cup Beef Broth

Directions:

1. Whisk together the butter, juice, broth, and gravy mix, in the IP.
2. Stir in the pepperoncini.
3. Place the beef inside and close the lid.
4. Set the Instant Pot to MANUAL.
5. Cook on HIGH for 40 minutes.
6. Do a natural pressure release.
7. Serve and enjoy!

(Calories 750| Total Fats 32g | Carbs: 12g | Protein 80g| Fiber 1g)

83. Feta Lamb Meatballs with Tomato Sauce

(Total Time: 25 MIN| Serves: 2)

Ingredients:

- 1 small Egg
- ¼ cup crumbled Feta Cheese
- ¼ tsp Oregano
- ¼ Onion, diced
- ½ pound ground Lamb
- ¼ cup Breadcrumbs
- 2 tbsp Olive Oil
- ½ tbsp chopped Mint
- ½ Bell Pepper, chopped
- 14 ounces canned diced Tomatoes
- 1 cup Water
- 1 tsp minced Garlic

Directions:

1. In a bowl, combine the meat, feta, breadcrumbs, mint, half of the garlic, and egg.
2. Make meatballs out of the mixture.
3. Heat half of the oil in the IP on SAUTE and add the meatballs.
4. Cook for a few minutes, until browned. Transfer to a plate.
5. Heat the remaining oil and saute the onions, peppers and remaining garlic for 3 minutes.

6. Add the tomatoes and place the meatballs inside.
7. Close the lid and cook on HIGH for 8 minutes.
8. Do a quick pressure release.
9. Serve and enjoy!

(Calories 380| Total Fats 17g | Carbs: 17 | Protein 39g| Fiber 1g)

84. Corned Beef with Cabbage

(Total Time: 60 MIN| Serves: 2)

Ingredients:

- 2/3 pound Corned Beef
- 2 Carrots, sliced
- 1 Celery Stalk, chopped
- 2 cups Water
- ½ Onion, chopped
- ½ tbsp favorite Seasoning
- 2/3 pound Red Cabbage, chopped
- ½ pound Potatoes, chopped

Directions:

1. Combine the beef, water, and seasoning, in the IP.
2. Close the lid and cook on HIGH for 40 minutes.
3. Do a quick pressure release.
4. Stir in the remaining ingredients and close the lid.
5. Cook for 6 more minutes on HIGH.
6. Do a quick pressure release.

7. Serve and enjoy!

(Calories 465| Total Fats 30g | Carbs: 18g | Protein 35g|

Fiber 3g)

85. Herbed Lamb with Tomatoes and Carrots

(Total Time: 50 MIN| Serves: 2)

Ingredients:

- 2 Lamb Shanks
- 1 tsp minced Garlic
- 1 Large Carrot, sliced
- 1 cup chopped Tomatoes
- 1 tbsp chopped Oregano
- 1 Thyme Sprig
- 1 Rosemary Sprig
- 1 tbsp chopped Basil
- 2 tbsp Olive Oil
- ½ Red Onion, sliced
- 1 ½ cups Beef Stock

Directions:

1. Heat the oil in the IP on SAUTE.
2. Add the onion and cook for 3 minutes.
3. Add the garlic and cook for one more.

4. Add the lamb shanks and cook them until browned on both sides.
5. Add the carrots and herbs, and pour the broth over.
6. Close the lid and choose the MANUAL cooking mode.
7. Cook for 20 minutes on HIGH.
8. Do a quick pressure release.
9. Add the tomatoes and close the lid again.
10. Cook on HIGH for 5-6 minutes more.
11. Release the pressure quickly and serve the lamb topped with the sauce.
12. Enjoy!

(Calories 700| Total Fats 38g | Carbs: 17g | Protein 65|

Fiber 1g)

86. Creamy Pork Sausage

(Total Time: 15 MIN| Serves: 2)

Ingredients:

- ½ pound Pork Sausage
- 1 ½ tsp minced Garlic
- 1 cup Milk
- 1 tbsp Butter
- 2 tbsp Flour

Directions:

1. Melt the butter in the IP on SAUTE and cook the garlic in it for about a minute.

2. Add the pork sausage and cook while breaking it with a wooden spoon, until it turns brown.
3. Whisk together the milk and flour and pout over.
4. Close the lid and select MANUAL.
5. Cook on HIGH for 6 minutes.
6. Do a quick pressure release.
7. Serve and enjoy!

(Calories 500| Total Fats 30g | Carbs: 17g | Protein 26g|

Fiber 1g)

87. Grape Jelly Meatballs

(Total Time: 35 MIN| Serves: 2)

Ingredients:

- ½ pound ground Beef
- 2 tbsp Cornstarch
- ¼ cup Grape Jelly
- ½ tsp Garlic Salt
- ½ tsp Paprika
- ½ cup mild Salsa
- 1 Egg

Directions:

1. In a bowl, combine the beef, cornstarch, salt, and egg.
2. Make meatballs out of the mixture.
3. Whisk the rest of the ingredients in the IP and drop the meatballs inside.

4. Close the lid and hit MANUAL.
5. Cook the meatballs on LOW for 30 minutes.
6. Do a quick pressure release.
7. Serve and enjoy!

(Calories 580| Total Fats 19g | Carbs: 26g | Protein 50g|

Fiber 1g)

88. Leg of Lamb with Potatoes

(Total Time: 30 MIN| Serves: 2)

Ingredients:

- 2 pounds Leg of Lamb
- 1 Bay Leaf
- ½ tsp Marjoram
- ½ tsp Sage
- 1 pound Potatoes, chopped
- ½ tsp Thyme
- 1 ½ tbsp Cornstarch
- 2 cups Beef Broth
- 2 tbsp Water
- 1 tsp minced Garlic
- 2 tbsp Olive Oil
- Salt and Pepper, to taste

Directions:

1. Combine the oil, herbs and spices, in a bowl.
2. Rub he mixture over the lamb.

3. Sear on all sides on SAUTE and then pour the broth around the meat.
4. Close the lid and cook for 40 minutes on HIGH.
5. Do a quick pressure release and add the potatoes.
6. Cook for 12 more minutes.
7. Release the pressure quickly and transfer the lamb and potatoes to a plate.
8. Whisk the cornstarch and water and stir the mixture into the IP.
9. Serve the gravy over the lamb and potatoes.
10. Cook on SAUTE for a few minutes.
11. Serve and enjoy!

(Calories 740| Total Fats 55g | Carbs: 19g | Protein 57g|

Fiber 1g)

89. Pork Cutlets in a Plum Sauce

(Total Time: 40 MIN| Serves: 2)

Ingredients:

- ½ pound Ground Pork
- 1 Egg
- 2 tbsp Breadcrumbs
- 1 tsp chopped Parsley
- ½ tsp Thyme
- 1 tbsp Cornstarch
- 1 tbsp Oil

- 1 tbsp Flour
- 6 ounces Plums, pitted
- 2 tsp minced Ginger
- 1 tbsp Sugar
- 1/3 cup Lemon Juice
- 3 tbsp Water

Directions:

1. In a bowl, combine the first 6 ingredients.
2. Form cutlets out of the mixture.
3. Heat the oil in the IP on SAUTE.
4. Add the cutlets and cook until they are browned on all sides.
5. In a blender, blend the remaining ingredients, until smooth.
6. Pour the plum sauce over the cutlets and close the lid.
7. Cook on HIGH for 8 minutes.
8. Do a quick pressure release.
9. Serve and enjoy!

(Calories 240| Total Fats 10g | Carbs: 15g | Protein 23g|

Fiber 1g)

90. Pork Tacos

(Total Time: 45 MIN| Serves: 2)

Ingredients:

- 6 ounces ground Pork

- 1 tbsp chopped Cilantro
- ¼ tsp Salt
- ¼ Red Onion, chopped
- 1 tbsp Butter
- ½ cup Tomato Sauce
- 2 Corn Tortillas
- 1/2 cup shredded Lettuce

Directions:

1. Combine the meat, onion, cilantro, butter, tomato sauce, and salt, in the Instant Pot.
2. Close the lid and cook on HIGH for 20 minutes.
3. Do a quick pressure release.
4. Divide the sauce between the tortillas and top with shredded lettuce.
5. Serve and enjoy!

(Calories 250| Total Fats 9g | Carbs: 20g | Protein 30g|

Fiber 1g)

91. Pot Roast in a Peach Sauce

(Total Time: 45 MIN| Serves: 2)

Ingredients:

- ¼ Onion, sliced
- 1 Garlic Clove, minced
- ¾ pound Beef Roast
- 2 cups Peach Juice

- 1 tbsp Cornstarch
- 1 tbsp Olive Oil

Directions:

1. Heat the oil in the IP on SAUTE.
2. Add the meat and cook until browned on all sides.
3. Add the onions and garlic and cook for two minutes.
4. Pour the juice over and close the lid.
5. Cook on MANUAL for 40 minutes.
6. Do a natural pressure release.
7. Transfer the meat t a plate.
8. Whish the cornstarch into the sauce and cook on SAUTE until thickened.
9. Serve the roast with the sauce.
10. Enjoy!

(Calories 325| Total Fats 11g | Carbs: 22g | Protein 38g|

Fiber 1g)

92. Gingery Lamb Shanks with Figs

(Total Time: MIN| Serves: 2)

Ingredients:

- 2 Lamb Shanks
- ¼ Onion, sliced
- 1 ½ cups Broth
- 1 tbsp Coconut Aminos

- 1 Garlic Clove, minced
- 1 tbsp minced Ginger
- 2 tsp Fish Sauce
- 4 dried Figs, chopped
- 2 tbsp Coconut Oil

Directions:

1. Melt half of the coconut oil in the IP on SAUTE.
2. Add the lamb and cook until browned on both sides. Transfer to a plate.
3. Melt the remaining oil and add the onions.
4. Cook for 2 minutes.
5. Add the garlic and ginger and cook for another minute.
6. Stir in the fish sauce, coconut aminos, figs, and broth.
7. Return the lamb to the plate and close the lid.
8. Cook on HIGH for 40 minutes.
9. Do a natural pressure release.
10. Serve the sauce over the lambs.
11. Enjoy!

(Calories 740| Total Fats 40g | Carbs: 30g | Protein 50g|

Fiber 3.3g)

93. Maple and Balsamic Beef

(Total Time: 35 MIN| Serves: 2)

Ingredients:

- ¾ pound Chuck Steak

- 1 tbsp Oil
- ¼ cup Balsamic Vinegar
- ½ cup Maple Syrup
- ¾ cup Bone Broth
- ½ tsp ground Ginger
- ½ tsp Salt

Directions:

1. Slice the beef into ½-inch thin slices.
2. Season with the salt and ginger.
3. Heat the oil in the IP and cook the beef until browned.
4. In a bowl, whisk together the remaining ingredients.
5. Pour over the beef and close the lid.
6. Set the Instant Pot to MANUAL.
7. Cook on HIGH for 25 minutes.
8. Do a quick pressure release.
9. Serve and enjoy!

(Calories 650| Total Fats 30g | Carbs: 36g | Protein 60g|

Fiber 0g)

94. Beef Lasagna

(Total Time: 40 MIN| Serves: 2)

Ingredients:

- ½ pounds Ricotta Cheese
- 1/2 pound Ground Beef
- 4 ounces Lasagna Noodles

- 10 ounces Pasta Sauce
- ¼ cup Water
- ¼ Onion, diced
- 1 Garlic Clove, minced
- 1 Egg
- 1 tbsp Oil
- 1/3 cup shredded Mozzarella Cheese
- ¼ cup grated Parmesan Cheese
- ½ tsp Italian Seasoning

Directions:

1. Heat the oil in the IP and add the onions.
2. Cook for 2 minute and then stir in the garlic.
3. Cook for 1 minute.
4. Add the beef and cook until browned.
5. Stir in the pasta sauce and water.
6. Transfers to a bowl.
7. In another bowl, combine the ricotta, egg, seasoning, and parmesan.
8. Pour some of the beef sauce at the bottom of the IP.
9. Arrange 1/3 of the noodles over and top with 1/3 of the sauce.
10. Place ½ of the ricotta over.
11. Repeat once more.
12. Top the final layer with the remaining beef sauce and sprinkle the mozzarella over.
13. Close the lid and cook on MANUAL for 7 minutes.
14. Do a quick pressure release.
15. Serve and enjoy!

(Calories 410| Total Fats 22g | Carbs: 247g | Protein 25g|
Fiber 3g)

95. Pork Fried Rice

(Total Time: 40 MIN| Serves: 2)

Ingredients:

- 1 cup Rice
- 1 Egg, beaten
- 1 Carrot, shredded
- ¼ Onion, diced
- ¼ cup diced Green Bens
- 5 ounces sliced Pork Loin
- 1 tbsp Soy Sauce
- 2 tbsp Oil
- 2 cups Water

Directions:

1. Heat half of the oil in the IP on SAUTE.
2. Add the pork and cook until browned.
3. Transfer the pork to a plate.
4. Heat the remaining oil and add onions and carrot.
5. Cook for 2 minutes.
6. Stir in the egg and cook until set.
7. Return the pork and stir in the rest of the ingredients.
8. Close the lid and cook on RICE for 10 minutes.
9. Do a quick pressure release.
10. Fluff with a fork before serving.
11. Serve and enjoy!

(Calories 550| Total Fats 2g | Carbs: 80g | Protein 22g|

Fiber 3g)

96. Meat-Stuffed Peppers

(Total Time: 35 MIN| Serves: 2)

Ingredients:

- 2 ounces ground Chilies, chopped
- 2 tbsp Butter
- ½ Onion, chopped
- 2 Large Bell Peppers
- 1 tsp minced Garlic
- ¼ cup Corn Kernels
- 1/3 cup shredded Cheddar Cheese
- ¼ pound ground Beef
- ¼ pound ground Pork
- ¼ tsp Oregano
- 1 ½ cups Water

Directions:

1. Melt the butter in the IP on SAUTE and add the onions.
2. Cook until they soften, about 5 minutes.
3. Add the garlic and cook for another minute.
4. Add the pork and beef and cook until they become browned.
5. Transfer the miture to a bowl and stir in the chillies, cheese, and corn.
6. Divide the mixture between the peppers.
7. Pour the water into the IP and lower the rack.
8. Place the peppers on the rack and close the lid.
9. Cook on HIGH for 10 minutes.
10. Do a quick pressure release.

11. Serve and enjoy!

(Calories 395| Total Fats 32g | Carbs: 17g | Protein 34g|

Fiber 1.5g)

Seafood Recipes

97. Steamed Tomato Mussels

(Total Time: 25 MIN| Serves: 2)

Ingredients:

- 2 pound Mussels
- 2 tbsp chopped Parsley
- 14 ounces canned stewed Tomatoes
- ¼ cup Dry White Wine
- 2 tsp minced Garlic
- 2 tsp Olive Oil
- 1 tsp Lemon Juice
- 8 ounces Clam Juice

Directions:

1. Scrub the mussels clean and pull off the membrane-like string. Set aside.
2. Heat the oil in the IP on SAUTE.
3. Add garlic and cook for 1 minute.
4. Stir in the wine, tomatoes, parsley, and juices.

5. Bring the mixture to a boil then place the mussels inside.
6. Cook for 4 minutes on MANUAL.
7. Release the pressure naturally.
8. Serve the mussels with the sauce.
9. Enjoy!

(Calories 295| Total Fats 9g | Carbs: 21g | Protein 25g|

Fiber 3.5g)

98. Honey and Orange Salmon

(Total Time: 12 MIN| Serves: 2)

Ingredients:

- 2 Salmon Fillets
- 2 tbsp Sriracha
- 2 tbsp Honey
- 1 tbsp Nanami Togarashi
- Juice of ½ Orange
- 1 tsp minced Ginger
- 1 tsp minced Garlic
- 1 ½ cups Water

Directions:

1. Pour the water into the Instant Pot and lower the trivet.
2. Mix together the juices, honey, sriracha, garlic, nanami togarashi, and ginger.

3. Place the salmon fillets in a greased baking dish and pour the sauce over.
4. Place the dish on the trivet and close the lid.
5. Cook for 6 minutes on POULTRY.
6. Do a quick pressure release.
7. Serve with the sauce. Enjoy!

(Calories 230| Total Fats 1g | Carbs: 23g | Protein 32g|

Fiber 1g)

99. White Bean Shrimp

(Total Time: 5 hours | Serves: 2)

Ingredients:

- 1/3 pound Shrimp, peeled and deveined
- 1 Bay Leaf
- 1 ½ cup Fish Stock
- 1/3 pound dried Beans
- 1 small Bell Pepper, diced
- ½ Onion, diced
- ½ Celery Stalk, diced
- 1 Garlic Clove, minced

Directions:

1. Place the beans in a bowl and fill with water.
2. Let soak for 4 hours.
3. Drain and rinse the beans.

4. Grease the IP with some cooking spray and set it to SAUTE.
5. Add the onions, peppers, and celery.
6. Cook for 3 minutes.
7. Add the garlic and cook for 1 minute.
8. Add the beans, stock, and bay leaf.
9. Cook for 15 minutes on POULTRY.
10. Do a quick pressure release and stir in the shrimp.
11. Close the lid and cook for another 6 minutes.
12. Release the pressure quickly and discard the bay leaf.
13. Serve and enjoy!

(Calories 530| Total Fats 25g | Carbs: 40g | Protein 35g|

Fiber 10g)

100. **Salmon with Tartar Sauce**

(Total Time: 12 MIN| Serves: 2)

Ingredients:

- 2 Salmon Fillets
- 1 Lemon, sliced
- ¼ cup White Wine
- ½ Onion, sliced
- 1 cup Water

Sauce:
- 1/3 cup Mayonnaise

- 1/3 cup Greek Yogurt
- 2 tbsp chopped Green Onions
- 3 tbsp Pickle Relish
- 1 tbsp Lemon Juice
- 1 tbsp chopped Capers
- 1 tbsp chopped Parsley
- 1 tsp Dijon Mustard
- Salt and Pepper, to taste

Directions:

1. Pour the water into the Instant Pot and lower the rack.
2. Arrange the salmon fillets on the rack and top with onion and lemon.
3. Drizzle with the white wine.
4. Close the lid and cook for 4 minutes on MANUAL.
5. Meanwhile, whisk together all of the sauce ingredients.
6. Do a quick pressure release.
7. Serve the salmon drizzled with the sauce.
8. Enjoy!

(Calories 495| Total Fats 39g | Carbs: 8g | Protein 24g|

Fiber 1g)

101. Jalapeno Cod with Olives and Tomatoes

(Total Time: 13 MIN| Serves: 2)

Ingredients:

- 2 Cod Fillets
- 8 Black Olives, chopped
- ½ Yellow Onion, chopped
- 3 tbsp Lime Juice
- 1 tbsp Olive Oil
- 1 Garlic Clove, minced
- 2 tbsp minced Jalapeno Rings
- 1 tbsp Brine from the Jalapeno Rings
- 1 tbsp chopped Capers
- ¼ cup Water

Directions:

1. Heat the oil in the IP on SAUTE.
2. Add the onion and cook for 3 minutes.
3. Stir in the garlic and cook for 30 seconds.
4. Arrange the cod fillets on top.
5. Combine the remaining ingredients in a bowl and pour over the cod.
6. Close the lid and cook on MANUAL for 5 minutes.
7. Do a quick pressure release. Serve and enjoy!

(Calories 640| Total Fats 35g | Carbs: 21g | Protein 60g|

Fiber 4g)

102. Shrimp Scampi and Rice

(Total Time: 20 MIN| Serves: 2)

Ingredients:

- ½ pound Frozen Shrimp
- 2 Garlic Cloves, minced
- Juice of 1 Lemon
- 2 tbsp Butter
- 2 tbsp Parsley
- ½ cup Rice
- 1 ¼ cup Water

Directions:

1. Place everything in your Instant Pot and stir to combine well.
2. Set the IP to POULTRY and cook for 6 minutes.
3. Press CANCEL and do a quick pressure release.
4. Let the shrimp cool down until safe to handle.
5. Peel off the shells and serve.
6. Enjoy!

(Calories 225| Total Fats 12g | Carbs: 14g | Protein 14g|

Fiber 2g)

103.Tuna Noodles

(Total Time: 8 MIN| Serves: 2)

Ingredients:

- 8 ounces Egg Noodles
- 1 can Tuna, drained
- 2 ounces shredded Cheddar
- ½ cup frozen Peas
- 1 ½ cups Water
- 2 ½ tbsp Breadcrumbs
- 14 ounces canned Mushroom Soup
- Salt and Pepper, to taste

Directions:

1. Pour the water into the Instant Pot and add the noodles.
2. Stir in the soup, tuna, and peas.
3. Close the lid and set the IP to POULTRY.
4. Cook for 5 minutes and then release the pressure quickly.
5. Add the cheese and breadcrumbs and stir to combine.
6. Cook on SAUTE for a minute.
7. Serve and enjoy!

(Calories 430| Total Fats 22g | Carbs: 41g | Protein 18g|

Fiber 2g)

104. Caramelized Tilapia

(Total Time: 55 MIN| Serves: 2)

Ingredients:

- 2 Tilapia Fillets
- 1 ½ tbsp Fish Sauce
- 1 Garlic Clove, minced
- 1 Spring Onion, minced
- 1 Red Chili, minced
- ¼ cup tbsp Sugar
- 1 cup Coconut Water
- Salt and Pepper, to taste
- 3 tbsp Water

Directions:

1. Combine the fish sauce and garlic with some salt and pepper, and brush over the tilapia.
2. Let sit for about half an hour.
3. Place the water and sugar in the Instant Pot and cook until caramelized on SAUTE.
4. Add the tilapia and pour the coconut water over.
5. Close the lid and cook on MANUAL for 10 minutes.
6. Do a quick pressure release.
7. Serve topped with chili and spring onions. Enjoy!

(Calories 150| Total Fats 2g | Carbs: 18g | Protein 21g| Fiber 1g)

105. Crunchy Tuna

(Total Time: 5 MIN| Serves: 2)

Ingredients:

- 1 can Tuna
- 2 tbsp Butter
- 1 cup crushed Saltine Crackers
- ½ tsp minced Garlic
- ½ cup grated Cheddar Cheese
- ¼ cup Water

Directions:

1. Melt the butter in your IP on saute.
2. Add the garlic and cook for 1 minute.
3. Stir in the tuna and the crackers and pour the broth over.
4. Close the lid and cook on HIGH for a minute.
5. Release the pressure quickly, stir in the cheese, and cook for an additional minute, also on HIGH.
6. Serve and enjoy!

(Calories 150| Total Fats 3g | Carbs: 13g | Protein 10g|

Fiber 0g)

106. Lobster Ziti Bake

(Total Time: 35 MIN| Serves: 2)

Ingredients:

- 4 ounces dried Ziti
- ¼ cup dry White Wine
- ½ tbsp Flour
- ½ tbsp chopped Tarragon
- ½ cup shredded Gruyere Cheese
- ½ tbsp Worcestershire Sauce
- ½ cup Half and Half
- 2 Lobster Tails
- 3 cups Water
- Salt and Pepper, to taste

Directions:

1. Combine the water, pasta, and lobster tails, in the Instant Pot.
2. Close the lid and cook on POULTRY for 10 minutes.
3. Release the pressure quickly and open the lid.
4. Drain the pasta and the lobster tails.
5. Let cool until safe to handle and scoop out the meat.
6. Wipe the IP clean and place the pasta and meat inside.
7. Stir in the remaining ingredients and close the lid.
8. Season with some salt and pepper.
9. Cook for a couple of minutes on SAUTE, or until thickened.
10. Serve and enjoy!

(Calories 440| Total Fats 15g | Carbs: 44g | Protein 28g| Fiber 1g)

107. Wrapped Fish with Potatoes

(Total Time: 15 MIN| Serves: 2)

Ingredients:

- 2 Fish Fillets (Salmon, Halibut, Tilapia, Cod, etc.)
- 1 Large Potato, sliced
- ½ Lemon, sliced
- ½ Onion, sliced
- 1 tbsp Olive Oil
- 1 ½ cups Water
- 1 tbsp chopped Parsley
- 1 ½ cup Water

Directions:

1. Get two pieces of parchment paper and place the fish fillets at the center of each of them.
2. Top the fish with potato slices, onion, lemon, and parsley.
3. Drizzle with the olive oil.
4. Wrap them up, and then wrap in aluminum foil.
5. Pour the water into the IP and lower the rack.
6. Place the fish packets on the rack and close the lid.
7. Cook for 5 minutes on HIGH.
8. Do a quick pressure release. Serve and enjoy!

(Calories 310| Total Fats 14g | Carbs: 9g | Protein 30g|

Fiber 3g)

108. Canned Salmon with Corn and Olives

(Total Time: 17 MIN| Serves: 2)

Ingredients:

- 1 can Salmon, drained
- 8 ounces dried Noodles
- ½ cup canned Corn
- ¼ cup grated Parmesan Cheese
- 4 cups Water
- ½ cup Heavy Cream
- 1 tbsp Butter
- ¼ cup chopped Black Olives

Directions:

1. Combine the noodles and water in the Instant Pot and close the lid.
2. Cook on HIGH for 5 minutes.
3. Do a quick pressure release and drain the pasta.
4. Wipe the pot clean and return the pasta to the IP.
5. Add the remaining ingredients and stir to combine well.
6. Cook on SAUTE for 3 minutes.
7. Serve and enjoy!

(Calories 456| Total Fats 18g | Carbs: 41g | Protein 17g|

Fiber 1.8g)

109. Simple Dijon Haddock

(Total Time: 5 MIN| Serves: 2)

Ingredients:

- 2 tbsp Haddock Fillets
- 1 ½ tbsp Dijon Mustard
- 1 ½ cup Water

Directions:

1. Pour the water into the Instant Pot.
2. Brush the mustard all over the fillets and place them in the steamer basket.
3. Lower the basket and close and seal the lid.
4. Set the IP to MANUAL and cook for 3 minutes on HIGH.
5. Do a quick pressure release.
6. Serve and enjoy!

(Calories 192| Total Fats 2g | Carbs: 0.3g | Protein 42g|

Fiber 0g)

110. Prawn and Egg Risotto

(Total Time: 40 MIN| Serves: 2)

Ingredients:

- 1 Egg, beaten
- 1/3 cup frozen Peas
- 2/3 cup Brown Rice
- 6 ounces pre-cooked Prawns
- 1 tbsp Sesame Oil
- 1 Garlic Clove, minced
- 1 ½ tbsp Soy Sauce
- 1/3 cup chopped Onion
- 2 cups Water

Directions:

1. Heat half of the oil in the IP on SAUTE.
2. Cook the egg until set. Transfer to a plate.
3. Heat the rest of the oil and add the onions.
4. Cook for 3 minutes and add the garlic.
5. Saute for another minute.
6. Stir in the rice, peas, soy sauce, and water.
7. Close the lid and cook for 10 minutes on MANUAL.
8. Do a quick pressure release.
9. Stir in the prawns and egg.
10. Cook on SAUTE for a few minutes.
11. Serve and enjoy!

(Calories 220| Total Fats 10g | Carbs: 22g | Protein 13g|

Fiber 1g)

111. Teriyaki Salmon

(Total Time: 202 MIN| Serves: 2)

Ingredients:

- 2 Salmon Fillets
- 1 tbsp Sweet Rice Wine
- ½ tbsp Sugar
- 1 Spring Onion, sliced
- ½ tbsp Sesame Oil
- 2 tbsp Spy Sauce
- 1 Bok Choy, cut in half
- 1 ounce dried Mushrooms
- 1 ½ cup Boiling Water

Directions:

1. Pour the water over to mushrooms and let them sit for a few minutes.
2. Place them in the Instant Pot and stir in the remaining ingredients, except for the salmon.
3. When combined, add the salmon fillets and close the lid.
4. Cook on HIGH for 4 minutes.
5. Release the pressure naturally.
6. Serve and enjoy!

(Calories 480| Total Fats 32g | Carbs: 17g | Protein 27g|

Fiber 3g)

112. Trout and Farro Salad

(Total Time: 55 MIN| Serves: 2)

Ingredients:

- 6 ounces chopped and cooked Trout
- ½ cup Farro
- 1 tbsp Dijon Mustard
- 1 ½ tbsp Lemon Juice
- ¼ cup Mayonnaise
- 2 tbsp Sour Cream
- ½ tsp Sugar
- 1/2 Fennel Bulb, shaved

Directions:

1. Place the farro in the Instant Pot and add just enough water to cover.
2. Close the lid and cook on MANUAL for 17 minutes.
3. Do a quick pressure release.
4. Place the fennel in a colander and drain the farro over it.
5. Transfer to a bowl and let cool for a few minutes.
6. Stir in the trout.
7. In a bowl, whisk together the remaining ingredients and drizzle over the salad. Serve and enjoy!

(Calories 460| Total Fats 20g | Carbs: 34g | Protein 30g|

Fiber 3.3g)

113. Creamy Shrimp Penne

(Total Time: 15 MIN| Serves: 2)

Ingredients:

- 6 ounces Penne Pasta
- ½ cup grated parmesan Cheese
- ¼ cup Heavy Cream
- 6 ounces peeled and deveined frozen Shrimp
- 2 cups Chicken Broth
- ½ Onion, chopped
- 1 tbsp Olive Oil
- 1 tsp Flour

Directions:

1. Heat the oil in the Instant Pot on SAUTE.
2. Add the onions and cook for 3 minutes.
3. Stir in the shrimp, pasta, and broth.
4. Close the lid and cook on HIH for 7 minutes.
5. Release the pressure quickly.
6. Whisk together the heavy cream and flour and pour over.
7. Stir in the parmesan and cook on SAUTE until the sauce is thickened. Serve and enjoy!

(Calories 508| Total Fats 20g | Carbs: 45g | Protein 33g|

Fiber 1g)

114. Orange and Gingery Fish

(Total Time: 20 MIN| Serves: 2)

Ingredients:

- 1 tbsp Honey
- 2 Fish Fillets
- 2 Spring Onions, chopped
- 2 tsp minced Ginger
- Juice and zest of ½ Orange
- 1 ¼ cup Fish Stock

Directions:

1. Brush the fillets with honey and place in the steamer basket.
2. Combine the rest of the ingredients, except the onions, in the IP and lower the basket.
3. Close the lid and cook on HIGH for 4-5 minutes.
4. Do a quick pressure release.
5. Serve the fish garnished with spring onions and drizzled with the cooking sauce.
6. Enjoy!

(Calories 290| Total Fats 2g | Carbs: 14.3g | Protein 40g| Fiber 3g)

115. Tuna Helper

(Total Time: 15 MIN| Serves: 2)

Ingredients:

- 1 can Tuna, drained
- 6 ounces dried Pasta
- ½ cup grated Cheese
- 2 cups Chicken Broth
- ¼ cup Heavy Cream

Directions:

10. Combine the water and pasta in the Instant Pot and close the lid.
11. Cook on HIGH for 7 minutes.
12. Do a quick pressure release.
13. Drain and stir in the remaining ingredients.
14. Set the IP to SAUTE and cook for 2 minutes.
15. Serve and enjoy!

(Calories 301| Total Fats 13g | Carbs: 31 | Protein 20g|

Fiber 1.5g)

116. Salmon and Tomato Pasta Casserole

(Total Time: 20 MIN| Serves: 2)

Ingredients:

- 1 can Salmon, drained
- 1 tbsp Capers
- 15 ounces canned diced Tomatoes
- 1 tbsp Olive Oil
- 2 cups Pasta
- Dry White Wine
- 1 tsp minced Garlic

Directions:

1. Set your IP to SAUTE.
2. Add the garlic and cook for a minute.
3. Stir in the pasta and tomatoes.
4. Fill the tomato can with white wine and pour over.
5. Close the lid and cook on MANUAL for 6 minutes.
6. Do a quick pressure release.
7. Stir in the remaining ingredients.
8. Serve and enjoy!

(Calories 650| Total Fats 20g | Carbs: 73g | Protein 25g|

Fiber 2.4g)

117. Shrimp Creole

(Total Time: 20 MIN| Serves: 2)

Ingredients:

- 14 ounces canned crushed Tomatoes
- ½ Onion, chopped
- 1 Celery Stalk, diced
- ½ pound Shrimp, peeled and deveined
- 1 tsp minced Garlic
- ½ Bell Pepper, diced
- 2 tsp Creole Seasoning
- 1 tbsp Tomato Paste
- 2 tsp Olive Oil

Directions:

1. Heat the oil in the IP on SAUTE.
2. Add the onions, peppers, and celery, and cook for 3 minutes.
3. Stir in the garlic and cook for another minute.
4. Whisk in the tomato paste and cook for an additional minute.
5. Stir in the remaining ingredients and close the lid.
6. Set the IP to MNUAL and cook on HIGH for 1 minute.
7. Do a quick pressure release. Serve and enjoy!

(Calories 260| Total Fats 4g | Carbs: 24g | Protein 31g|

Fiber 5g)

118. Seafood and Cranberry Plov

(Total Time: 40 MIN| Serves: 2)

Ingredients:

- 8 ounces frozen Seafood Blend
- ½ Onion, chopped
- ½ Lemon, sliced
- 1 ½ tbsp Butter
- 1 Large Carrot, shredded
- ¾ cup Basmati Rice
- ½ Bell Pepper, sliced
- ¼ cup dried Cranberries
- 1 ½ cups Water

Directions:

1. Melt the butter in the IP and add the onions, pepper, and carrots. Saute for 3 minutes.
2. Add the garlic and cook for 1 mor minute.
3. Stir in the remaining ingredients and close the lid.
4. Set the IP to RICE and cook for 7 minutes.
5. Wait 5 minutes before doing a quick pressure release.
6. Serve and enjoy!

(Calories 430| Total Fats 7g | Carbs: 65g | Protein 22g|

Fiber 3g)

119. Pesto Farfale

(Total Time: 10 MIN| Serves: 2)

Ingredients:

- 7 ounces pasta Farfale
- 2/3 cup Pesto Sauce
- 3 cups Water
- ½ cup halved Cherry Tomatoes
- 1 tbsp chopped Basil
- 2 tbsp grated Parmesan Cheese

Directions:

1. Combine the pasta and water in the IP and close the lid.
2. Cook for 7 minutes on HIGH.
3. DO a quick pressure release.
4. Drain and return to the IP.
5. Stir in the cherry tomatoes and pesto and cook for 1 more minute.
6. Divide between two plates.
7. Top with basil and parmesan.
8. Serve and enjoy!

(Calories 395| Total Fats 10g | Carbs: 40g | Protein 8g|

Fiber 1g)

120. Spinach and Mushroom Risotto

(Total Time: 25 MIN| Serves: 2)

Ingredients:

- ¼ Onion, diced
- 1 cup Spinach
- 2 tbsp Lemon Juice
- 4 ounces Mushrooms, sliced
- ¼ cup dry White Wine
- 1 tbsp Butter
- 2/3 cup Arborio Rice
- 1 tbsp Nutritional Yeast
- 2 ½ cups Vegetable Broth
- 1 tbsp Olive Oil

Directions:

1. Heat the oil in the IP on SAUTE.
2. Add the onions and cook for 3 minutes.
3. Stir in the rice, and mushrooms, and cook for 2 minutes.
4. Add broth and wine and stir to combine.
5. Close the lid and set the IP to MANUAL.
6. Cook on HIGH for 6 minutes.
7. Do a quick pressure release.
8. Stir in the butter, spinach, and yeast.
9. Let sit for 2 minutes before serving.
10. Enjoy!

(Calories 320| Total Fats 8g | Carbs: 45g | Protein 10g| Fiber 6g)

121. Stuffed Eggplant

(Total Time: 50 MIN| Serves: 2)

Ingredients:

- 2 Eggplants
- ½ pound Mushrooms, chopped
- ½ cup diced Celery
- 1 tbsp Oil
- ½ Onion, diced
- ¾ cup grated Cheddar Cheese
- 1 tbsp chopped Parsley
- 1 ½ cups Water

Directions:

1. Cut the eggplants in half lengthwise and scoop out the flesh. Reserve it.
2. Pour the water into the IP and lower the rack.
3. Place the eggplants on the rack and drizzle with oil.
4. Close the lid and cook on HIGH for 5 minutes.
5. In a bowl, combine the remaining ingredients, including the reserved flesh.
6. Do a quick pressure release and divide the mixture between the eggplants.
7. Return the eggplants to the rack and cook for 10 minutes on HIGH.
8. Release the pressure quickly.
9. Serve and enjoy!

(Calories 175| Total Fats 7g | Carbs: 25g | Protein 6g| Fiber 3g)

122. Veggie Patties

(Total Time: 30 MIN| Serves: 2)

Ingredients:

- ½ Zucchini, grated
- 1 Carrot, grated
- 1 cup Broccoli Florets
- 1 cup Sweet Potato cubes
- 2 tbsp Olive Oil
- ½ tsp Turmeric
- 1 ½ cups Cauliflower Florets
- 2/3 cup Veggie Broth

Directions:

1. Heat half of the oil in the IP on SAUTE.
2. Add the onions and cook for 3 minutes.
3. Add carrots and cook for another minute.
4. Stir in the potatoes and broth and close the lid.
5. Cook for 6 minutes on HIGH.
6. Do a quick pressure release.
7. Stir in the remaining vegetables.
8. Close the lid and cook for 3 more minutes.
9. Release the pressure quickly and mash the veggies with a potato masher.
10. Let cool until safe to handle and shape into patties.
11. Wipe the pot clean and heat the remaining oil in it.
12. Add the patties and cook on SAUTE until golden.
13. Serve and enjoy!

(Calories 220| Total Fats 7g | Carbs: 34g | Protein 4g|

Fiber 6.5g)

123. Leafy Risotto

(Total Time: 20 MIN| Serves: 2)

Ingredients:

- 2/3 cup Arborio Rice
- ½ cup chopped Spinach
- ½ cup chopped Kale
- ¼ cup grated Parmesan Cheese
- ¼ cup diced Onion
- 1 tsp minced Garlic
- 2 ½ cups Veggie Broth
- 1 tbsp Oil
- 1 tbsp Butter

Directions:

1. Heat the oil in the IP on SAUTE.
2. Add the onions and cook for 3 minutes.
3. Add garlic and cook for 1 minute.
4. Stir in the rice and cook for an additional minute.
5. Pour the broth over, stir to combine, and close the lid.
6. Cook on RICE for 6 minutes.
7. Do a quick pressure release.
8. Drain if there is excess liquid.
9. Stir in the butter, parmesan, and greens.

10. Serve after 2 minutes.
11. Enjoy!

(Calories 272| Total Fats 11g | Carbs: 140g | Protein 6g|

Fiber 3g)

124. Spaghetti "Bolognese"

(Total Time: 25 MIN| Serves: 2)

Ingredients:

- 2 cups cooked Spaghetti
- 1 tbsp Tomato Paste
- ½ cup Cauliflower Florets
- 1 tbsp Balsamic Vinegar
- 5 ounces Mushrooms
- 14 ounces canned diced Tomatoes
- 1 tsp dried Basil
- ¼ tsp Oregano
- 1 tbsp Agave Nectar
- ¼ cup chopped Eggplant

Directions:

1. Place the cauliflower, eggplants, and mushrooms, in your food processor. Pulse until ground.
2. Transfer the mixture to the Instant Pot.
3. Stir in the rest of the ingredients, except the spaghetti.
4. Close the lid and cook on HIGH for 6 minutes.
5. Do a quick pressure release.

6. Stir in the spaghetti. Serve and enjoy!

(Calories 360| Total Fats 2.3g | Carbs: 72g | Protein 14g|

Fiber 8g)

125. Bean and Rice Bake

(Total Time: 40 MIN| Serves: 2)

Ingredients:

- ½ cup Beans, soaked and rinsed
- 2 ½ cups Water
- 1 cup Brown Rice
- 1 tsp Chili Powder
- 3 ounces Tomato Sauce
- 1 Garlic Clove, minced
- 1 tsp Onion Powder
- ¼ tsp Salt

Directions:

1. Place all of the ingredients in your IP.
2. Close the lid and set it to POULTRY.
3. Cook for 27 minutes.
4. Do a quick pressure release.
5. Serve and enjoy!

(Calories 320| Total Fats 2g | Carbs: 63g | Protein 6g|

Fiber 9g)

126. Sweet Potato, Broccoli & Tofu in a Tamari Sauce

(Total Time: 15 MIN| Serves: 2)

Ingredients:

- ½ pound Tofu, cubed
- 2 tsp Rice Vinegar
- 1 tbsp Tahini
- 2 tbsp Tamari
- 1 Garlic Clove, minced
- 1/3 cup Veggie Stock
- 1 cup Onion Slices
- 1 tbsp Sriracha
- 2 tsp Sesame Oil
- 1 tbsp Sesame Seeds
- 1 cup Broccoli Florets
- ½ cup diced Sweet Potato

Directions:

1. Heat the oil in the IP.
2. Add the sweet potatoes and onions and cook for 3 minutes.
3. Add garlic and cook for a minute.
4. Stir in the tofu, tamari, vinegar, and broth.
5. Close the lid and cook for 2 minutes on HIGH.
6. So a quick pressure release and stir in the broccoli.
7. Cook for another 2 minutes.

8. Release the pressure quickly, again, and stir in the sriracha.
9. Serve and enjoy!

(Calories 250| Total Fats 12g | Carbs: 22g | Protein 17g|

Fiber 2g)

127. Carrot and Sweet Potato Medley

(Total Time: 30 MIN| Serves: 2)

Ingredients:

- ½ Onion, chopped
- 1 pound Baby Carrots, halved
- 1 pound Sweet Potatoes, cubed
- 2 tbsp Olive Oil
- ½ tsp Italian Seasoning
- 1 cup Vegetable Broth
- ¼ tsp Garlic Salt

Directions:

1. Heat the oil in the IP on SAUTE.
2. Add the onions and cook for about 3-4 minutes.
3. Add the carrots and cook for another 3-4 minutes.
4. Stir in the remaining ingredients.
5. Close the lid and set the IP to MANUAL.
6. Cook for 8 minutes on HIGH.
7. Serve and enjoy!

(Calories 413| Total Fats 7g | Carbs: 74g | Protein 7g|

Fiber 12g)

128. Fruity Wild Rice Casserole with Almonds

(Total Time: 55 MIN| Serves: 2)

Ingredients:

- 1/3 cup dried Fruit
- 2 tbsp Apple Juice
- ½ Pear, chopped
- 1 Apple, chopped
- ½ tbsp Maple Syrup
- ¼ cup Slivered Almonds
- ¾ cup Wild Rice
- 2 cups Water
- 1 tsp Oil
- Pinch of Cinnamon

Directions:

1. Place the rice and water in the IP and close the lid.
2. Cook on HIGH for 20 minutes.
3. Meanwhile combine the dried fruit and apple juice and let sit for 20 minutes.
4. Drain the fruits and chop them.
5. Do a quick pressure release and stir in the remaining ingredients.

6. Close the lid again and cook for 2 minutes on HIGH.
7. Serve and enjoy!

(Calories 410| Total Fats 5g | Carbs: 70g | Protein 9g|

Fiber 19g)

129. Basil Risotto

(Total Time: 30 MIN| Serves: 2)

Ingredients:

- ¼ Onion, chopped
- 1 cup Rice
- 2 ¼ cup Chicken Broth
- 2 tbsp grated Parmesan Cheese
- 1 tbsp Oil
- A handful of Basil, chopped

Directions:

1. Set your Instant Pot to SAUTE and heat the oil in it.
2. Add the onions and cook for 2 minutes.
3. Add the rice and cook for an additional minute.
4. Pour the broth over, stir to combine, and close the lid.
5. Cook on RICE for 10 minutes.
6. Do a quick pressure release.
7. Drain if there is excess liquid.
8. Stir in the basil and serve topped with parmesan.
9. Enjoy!

(Calories 510| Total Fats 7g | Carbs: 80g | Protein 12| Fiber
20g)

130 Wheat Berries with Tomatoes

(Total Time: 45 MIN| Serves: 2)

Ingredients:

- ¾ cup Wheat Berries
- 1 tbsp Butter
- 8 ounces diced canned Tomatoes
- ½ cup Chicken Broth

Directions:

1. Melt the butter in your Instant Pot on SAUTE.
2. Add the wheat berries and cook for about 2 minutes.
3. Stir in the remaining ingredients.
4. Close the lid and set the IP to MANUAL.
5. Cook on HIGH for 25 minutes.
6. Do a natural pressure release.
7. Serve and enjoy!

(Calories 140| Total Fats 7g | Carbs: 15 g | Protein 4g|

Fiber 4g)

131. Black Bean Hash

(Total Time: 10 MIN| Serves: 2)

Ingredients:

- 2 cups cubed Sweet Potatoes
- ½ cup chopped Onions
- 1 tsp Chili Powder
- 1/3 cup Veggie Broth
- 1 cup canned Black Beans, drained
- ¼ cup chopped Scallions
- 1 tbsp Olive Oil

Directions:

1. Heat the oil in your IP on SAUTE.
2. Add the onions and cook for 3 minutes.
3. Add the rest of the ingredients.
4. Give it a good stir to combine well.
5. Close the lid and set the IP to MANUAL.
6. Cook for 3 minutes on HIGH.
7. Release the pressure quickly.
8. Serve and enjoy!

(Calories 266| Total Fats 9g| Carbs: 28g | Protein 5g|

Fiber 6g)

132. Rich Veggie Risotto

(Total Time: 30 MIN| Serves: 2)

Ingredients:

- 1 cup Arborio Rice
- 1 Carrot, shredded
- 1 tbsp Olive Oil
- 2 tbsp Butter
- ¼ Onion, chopped
- ¼ cup Heavy Cream
- 5 ounces Mushrooms, sliced
- 2 tbsp grated Parmesan Cheese
- 1 Bell Pepper, diced
- 1 2/3 cup Veggie Stock
- ½ tsp minced Garlic

Directions:

1. Set your Instant Pot to SAUTE and heat the oil in it.
2. Add the onions and peppers and cook for 3 minutes.
3. Add garlic and cook for one more minute.
4. Stir in the carrots and mushrooms. Cook for 3 minutes.
5. Stir in the rice and broth and close the lid.
6. Choose the MANUAL cooking mode.
7. Cook for 10 minutes on HIGH.
8. Do a quick pressure release.
9. Stir in the heavy cream and butter.
10. Sprinkle with parmesan cheese.
11. Serve and enjoy!

(Calories 300| Total Fats 4g | Carbs: 47g | Protein 5g|

Fiber 12g)

133. Instant Mac and Cheese

(Total Time: 10 MIN| Serves: 2)

Ingredients:

- 1 tbsp Butter
- 2 cups Elbow Macaroni
- ½ cup Milk
- 2 cups Chicken Stock
- ¾ cup shredded Pepper Jack Cheese
- 2 tbsp Parmesan Cheese
- ¼ tsp Pepper
- Pinch of Salt

Directions:

1. Place all of the ingredients, except the cheese, in the IP.
2. Stir to combine well.
3. Close the lid and choose MANUAL.
4. Cook on HIGH for 7 minutes.
5. Do a quick pressure release.
6. Stir in the shredded cheese and wait to melt before serving.
7. Sprinkle with the parmesan cheese.
8. Serve and enjoy!

(Calories 650| Total Fats 49g | Carbs: 48g | Protein 30g| Fiber 5g)

134. Caprese Pasta

(Total Time: 20 MIN| Serves: 2)

Ingredients:

- 2 cups Penne Pasta
- 2 tsp minced Garlic
- ½ cup halved Grape Tomatoes
- A handful of Basil Leaves
- ½ cup Mozzarella Balls
- 8 ounces Tomato Sauce
- ¼ Onion, diced
- 1 tbsp Balsamic Vinegar
- 2 cups Water
- 1 tbsp Olive Oil

Directions:

1. Heat the oil in the IP on SAUTE.
2. Add the garlic and cook for a minute.
3. Add the sauce, tomatoes, pasta, water, and half of the basil.
4. Stir to combine and close the lid.
5. Set the IP to MANUAL and cook for 5 minutes on HIGH.
6. Do a natural pressure release.
7. Stir in the mozzarella and remaining basil.
8. Serve and enjoy!

(Calories 480| Total Fats 9g | Carbs: 80g | Protein 18g|

Fiber 8g)

135. Nutty and Minty Barley Salad

(Total Time: 3 hours and 30 MIN| Serves: 2)

Ingredients:

- 2/3 cup Barley
- ¼ cup chopped Pine Nuts
- 2 tbsp Sparkling Wine
- ¼ tsp Onion Powder
- 1 tsp Lemon Zest
- 2 tbsp chopped Mint
- 1 Spring Onion, chopped
- ¼ tsp Red Pepper Flakes
- 1 tbsp Olive Oil
- 2 cups Water

Directions:

1. Combine the water and barley in the IP and close the lid.
2. Cook on RICE for 17 minutes.
3. Do a quick pressure release.
4. Stir in the remaining ingredients.
5. Transfer the barley to a bowl and cover.
6. Refrigerate for 3 hours.
7. Divide between 2 bowls.
8. Sprinkle with some grated cheese, if desired.
9. Serve and enjoy!

(Calories 370| Total Fats 14g | Carbs: 54g | Protein 8g|

Fiber 18g)

136. Cheesy Kamut

(Total Time: 20 MIN| Serves: 2)

Ingredients:

- 2/3 cup Kamut
- 1 Bell Pepper, chopped
- ½ cup halved Cherry Tomatoes
- 2 tbsp Parmesan Cheese
- ¼ cup Haloumi Cheese, chopped
- 2 tbsp Olive Oil
- 1 tsp Honey
- 2 tsp Lemon Juice
- Pinch of Salt
- 2 cups Water

Directions:

1. Combine the kamut and water in your IP.
2. Close the lid and set the IP on SOUP.
3. Cook for about 25 minutes.
4. Do a quick pressure release.
5. Stir in the veggies and cheeses.
6. In a bowl, whisk together the salt, lemon juice, oil, and honey.
7. Drizzle the vinaigrette over the salad. Serve and enjoy!

(Calories 280| Total Fats 13g | Carbs: 32g | Protein 8g|

Fiber 11g)

137. Black Eyed Pea Lunch Cakes

(Total Time: 45 MIN| Serves: 2)

Ingredients:

- 1 cup Black Eyed Peas, soaked and rinsed
- 1 Onion, chopped
- 1 Roasted Red Pepper
- 1 tbsp Tomato Paste
- ¼ cup Veggie Broth
- 1 tsp Old Bay Seasoning

Directions:

1. Place the drained beans in a food processor.
2. Place in a bowl with water and remove the skin.
3. Drain and return to the food processor.
4. Add the remaining ingredients. Pulse until smooth.
5. Grease two large ramekins and divide the mixture between them.
6. Wrap the ramekins in foil.
7. Pour some water into your IP (about 1-2 cups) and lower the trivet.
8. Place the ramekins on the trivet and close the lid.
9. Cook for 30 minutes on POULTRY.
10. Do a quick pressure release. Serve and enjoy!

(Calories 320| Total Fats 2g | Carbs: 19g | Protein 18g|

Fiber 5g)

138. Lentil Sloppy Joe's

(Total Time: 55 MIN| Serves: 2)

Ingredients:

- 1 cup Green Lentils
- 1 Red Bell Pepper, chopped
- ¼ Onion, chopped
- 1 tbsp Soy Sauce
- 1 tbsp Coconut Sugar
- 1 tbsp Olive Oil
- 1 tbsp Dijon Mustard
- 2 cups Veggie Broth
- 8 ounces canned crushed Tomatoes

Directions:

1. Heat the oil in the IP on SAUTE.
2. Add the onions and peppers and cook for 3 minutes.
3. Stir in the remaining ingredients.
4. Close the lid and select MANUAL.
5. Cook for 22 minutes on HIGH.
6. Do a natural pressure release.
7. Serve and enjoy!

(Calories 350| Total Fats 6.5g | Carbs: 75g | Protein 18g|

Fiber 7g)

139. Eggplant Burgers

(Total Time: 25 MIN| Serves: 2)

Ingredients:

- ½ Eggplant, cut in half
- 1 tbsp Mustard
- 1 tbsp Olive Oil
- ¼ cup Panko Breadcrumbs
- 1 cup Water

Directions:

1. Pour the water into the IP and place the eggplants inside.
2. Close the lid and cook for 2 minutes on HIGH.
3. Drain the liquid and pat the eggplants dry with some paper towels.
4. Brush with mustard and coat with breadcrumbs.
5. Wipe the IP clean and heat the oil in it.
6. Add the burgers and cook until golden on all sides.
7. Serve in buns.
8. Serve and enjoy!

(Calories 130| Total Fats 2g | Carbs: 9g | Protein 2g| Fiber 1g)

140. Vegetarian Shepherd's Pie

(Total Time: 17 MIN| Serves: 2)

Ingredients:

- ½ cup diced Onion
- ¼ cup diced Celery
- 1 tbsp Olive Oil
- ¼ cup diced Turnip
- ½ cup diced Tomatoes
- ½ cup grated Potatoes
- ¼ cup diced Carrots
- 1 cup cooked and mashed Cauliflower
- 1 cup Water
- 1 cup Vegie Broth

Directions:

1. Heat the oil in the IP on SAUTE.
2. Add the onions, celery, and carrots. Saute for about 3 minutes.
3. Add the potatoes and turnips and pour the broth over.
4. Close the lid and cook on HIGH for 7 minutes.
5. Do a quick pressure release.
6. Grease a baking dish with cooking spray and transfer the drained veggies to it.
7. Top with the mashed cauliflower.
8. Pour the water into the IP and lower the trivet.
9. Place the baking dish on the trivet and close the lid.
10. Cook on HIGH for 5 minutes.
11. Release the pressure quickly.

12. Serve and enjoy!

(Calories 224| Total Fats 14g | Carbs: 6g | Protein 16g|

Fiber 0g)

141. Garlic Green Beans

(Total Time: 20 MIN| Serves: 2)

Ingredients:

- 1 /2 pound Green Beans
- 1 tbsp White Wine Vinegar
- 1 ½ tbsp Olive Oil
- 1 cup Water
- 2 tsp minced Garlic
- 1 tbsp chopped Parsley
- Salt and Pepper, to taste

Directions:

1. Place the green beans in the Instant Pot and pour the water rover.
2. Close the lid and set the IP to MANUAL.
3. Cook for one minute on HIGH.
4. Do a quick pressure release.
5. Drain and transfer to a bowl.
6. In a bowl, whisk together the remaining ingredients.
7. Pour over the beans.
8. Serve and enjoy!

(Calories 144| Total Fats 10g | Carbs: 9g | Protein 3.5g| Fiber 3g)

142. Buttery Onions

(Total Time: 50 MIN| Serves: 2)

Ingredients:

- 1 Large Onion, sliced
- 3 tbsp Butter
- ¼ cup Water
- ¼ tsp Salt

Directions:

1. Melt the butter in the IP and add the onions.
2. Season with salt and saute for good 7, 8 minutes.
3. Pour the water over and close the lid.
4. Se the IP to MANUAL and cook on HIGH for 15 minutes.
5. Do a quick pressure release.
6. Serve and enjoy!

(Calories 20| Total Fats 1.5g | Carbs: 2g | Protein 0g| Fiber 0g)

143. Sweet Carrot Puree

(Total Time: 25 MIN| Serves: 2)

Ingredients:

- 1 tbsp Butter
- 1 tbsp Honey
- Pinch of Salt

- 1 tsp Brown Sugar
- ¾ pound Carrots, chopped
- 1 ½ cups Water

Directions:

1. Pour the water in the instant pot.
2. Place the chopped carrots in the steamer basket.
3. Lower the basket and close the lid.
4. Cook for 4 minutes on HIGH.
5. Press CANCEL and stir in the rest of the ingredients.
6. Blend with a hand blender until smooth.
7. Serve and enjoy!

(Calories 45| Total Fats 0g | Carbs: 11g | Protein 1g| Fiber 1g)

144. Sour and Tangy Cabbage and Applesauce

(Total Time: 20 MIN| Serves: 2)

Ingredients:

- 1 tsp minced Garlic
- 1 tbsp Apple Cider Vinegar
- ½ cup Applesauce
- 3 cups chopped Cabbage
- 1 tbsp Olive Oil
- ¼ cup minced Onion
- 1 cup Water

Directions:

1. Heat the olive oil in the Instant Pot on SAUTE.
2. Add the onions and saute them for about 3 minutes.
3. Add garlic and then cook for another minute.
4. Add the rest of the ingredients to the IP.
5. Stir to combine and seal the lid.
6. Cook on MANUAL for 10 minutes.
7. Do a quick pressure release.
8. Serve and enjoy!

(Calories 105| Total Fats 4g | Carbs: 18g | Protein 2g|

Fiber 2.4g)

145. Instant Turmeric Carrots

(Total Time: 15 MIN| Serves: 2)

Ingredients:

- ½ pound Carrots, peeled
- 1 tsp Turmeric Powder
- 1 ½ cups Water
- 1 tbsp Butter, melted
- ¼ tsp Salt
- Pinch of Pepper

Directions:

1. Chop the carrots into thirds and place in the steamer basket.

2. Pour the water into the IP and lower the basket.
3. Close the lid and cook for 4 minutes on HIGH.
4. Do a quick pressure release.
5. Season with the salt, pepper, and turmeric.
6. Drizzle the butter over.
7. Serve and enjoy!

(Calories 48| Total Fats 2g | Carbs: 11g | Protein 1g| Fiber 1g)

146. Boiled Sweet Potatoes

(Total Time: 25 MIN| Serves: 2)

Ingredients:

- 2 Sweet Potatoes
- 2 cups Water

Directions:

1. Wash the potatoes, peel, and prick them.
2. Place in the Instant Pot's basket.
3. Pour the water into the pot and then lower the basket.
4. Close the lid and cook on HIGH for 10 minutes.
5. Do a quick pressure release.
6. Serve and enjoy!

(Calories 103| Total Fats 0.2g | Carbs: 24g | Protein 2.3g|
Fiber 4g)

147. Turmeric Couscous

(Total Time: 10 MIN| Serves: 2)

Ingredients:

- 4 ounces Couscous
- 1 tsp Turmeric Powder
- 1 tbsp Butter
- 1 cup Chicken Broth
- Salt and Pepper, to taste

Directions:

1. Melt the butter in the IP on SAUTE.
2. Add turmeric and couscous and cook for a minute.
3. Pour the broth over, give it a stir, and close the lid.
4. Choose MANUAL and set the cooking time for 5 minutes at HIGH.
5. Do a quick pressure release.
6. Season with salt and pepper.
7. Serve and enjoy!

(Calories 201| Total Fats 2.3g | Carbs: 35g | Protein 7g|

Fiber 8g)

148. Garlicky Polenta

(Total Time: 30 MIN| Serves: 2)

Ingredients:

- 1 ½ cups Hot Water
- ¼ cup chopped Cilantro
- 1 cup Corn Meal
- 2 cups Vegetable Broth
- ½ tsp Chili Powder
- 3 tsp minced Garlic
- ¼ tsp Paprika

Directions:

1. Add a splash of the hot water in your IP and combine the garlic and spices.
2. Cook for a minute.
3. Add the remaining ingredients and stir to combine well.
4. Close the lid and cook on HIGH for 10 minutes.
5. Let the pressure drop naturally. This shouldn't take longer than 10 minutes.
6. Serve and enjoy!

(Calories 200| Total Fats 8g | Carbs: 13g | Protein 14g|

Fiber 4g)

149. Steamed Soy Asparagus

(Total Time: 20 MIN| Serves: 2)

Ingredients:

- ½ pound Asparagus Sears, trimmed
- 1 tbsp Olive Oil
- 2 tbsp Soy Sauce
- ¼ tsp Garlic Powder
- ½ tsp Oyster Sauce
- ¼ tsp Onion Powder
- Salt and Pepper, to taste
- 1 ½ cups Water

Directions:

1. Pour the water into the Instant Pot.
2. Place the trimmed asparagus in the steamer basket.
3. Lower the basket into the water and close the lid.
4. Select the STEAM cooking mode.
5. Cook for 2 minutes.
6. Do a quick pressure release.
7. Whisk the remaining ingredients in a small bowl and drizzle over the asparagus.
8. Serve and enjoy!

(Calories 96| Total Fats 7.4g | Carbs: 7g | Protein 3g|

Fiber 1.3g)

150. Basic White Rice

(Total Time: 15 MIN| Serves: 2)

Ingredients:

- ½ cup Basmati Rice
- 1 1/3 cup Water
- Salt and Pepper, to taste

Directions:

1. Combine the rice and water in the IP.
2. Close the lid and choose the MANUAL cooking mode.
3. Cook the rice on LOW for 8 minutes.
4. Do a quick pressure release.
5. Fluff the rice with a fork.
6. Season with some salt and pepper.
7. Serve as desired and enjoy!

(Calories 225| Total Fats 0.5g | Carbs: 47g | Protein 4g|

Fiber 7g)

151. Ham and Pea Side Bowl

(Total Time: 40 MIN| Serves: 2)

Ingredients:

- 2 ounces diced Ham
- 1/3 pound Peas
- 2 ¼ cup Stock

Directions:

1. Place all of the ingredients in the Instant Pot.
2. Stir to combine well.
3. Close the lid and cook on HIGH for 22 minutes.
4. Do a natural pressure release.
5. Serve and enjoy!

(Calories 180| Total Fats 5g | Carbs: 10g | Protein 13g|

Fiber 3g)

152. Brussel Sprouts with Bacon and Cheese

(Total Time: 35 MIN| Serves: 2)

Ingredients:

- 2 cups Brussel Sprouts
- 1 ½ Bacon Slices, chopped
- 2/3 tbsp Balsamic Vinegar
- 2 tbsp crumbled Goat Cheese
- 2 tbsp Water

Directions:

1. Add the bacon pieces to your Instant Pot.
2. Set it to SAUTE and cook until crispy.
3. Stir in the balsamic, water, and Brussel sprouts.
4. Cook on SAUTE for 6 minutes, stirring occasionally.

5. Transfer to a serving bowl and top with goat cheese.
6. Serve and enjoy!

(Calories 140| Total Fats 8g | Carbs: 8g | Protein 10g| Fiber 2g)

153. Maple-Glazed Carrots

(Total Time: 10 MIN| Serves: 2)

Ingredients:

- ½ pound Carrots
- 1 tbsp Maple Syrup
- 1 tbsp melted Butter
- 1 tbsp Raisins
- ½ cup Water

Directions:

1. Place the water, raisins, and carrots in the Instant Pot.
2. Stir to combine and close the lid.
3. Select MANUAL and cook on LOW for 4 minutes.
4. Do a quick pressure release.
5. Drain and transfer to a bowl.
6. Whisk together the butter and maple.
7. Brush over the carrots.
8. Serve and enjoy!

(Calories 80| Total Fats 1g | Carbs: 16g | Protein 1g| Fiber 3g)

154. Zucchini and Mushroom Side

(Total Time: 20 MIN| Serves: 2)

Ingredients:

- 1 Zucchini, sliced
- 1 tbsp Olive Oil
- 1/3 cup diced Onion
- 4 ounces Mushrooms, sliced
- 5 ounces canned diced Tomatoes
- 1 tbsp chopped Basil
- 1 Garlic Clove, minced

Directions:

1. Heat the oil in your IP on SAUTE.
2. Add onion and cook for 2 minutes.
3. Stir in the mushrooms and cook for another 2 minutes.
4. Add garlic and cook just for a minute.
5. Add the rest of the ingredients and stir to combine well.
6. Close the lid and set the IP to MANUAL.
7. Cook on LOW for 2 minutes.
8. Let the pressure drop on its own.
9. Serve and enjoy!

(Calories 96| Total Fats 3g | Carbs: 15g | Protein 6g| Fiber 2g)

155. Tomato and Tofu Side

(Total Time: 10 MIN| Serves: 2)

Ingredients:

- ½ Tofu Block, cubed
- ½ can diced Tomatoes
- 1 tsp Italian Seasoning
- 1 tbsp chopped jarred Banana Pepper Rings
- ¼ cup Veggie Broth

Directions:

1. Dump all of the ingredients into your IP.
2. Stir to combine everything well.
3. Close and seal the lid of the IP and choose the MANUAL mode.
4. Set the cooking temperature to 4 minutes.
5. Cook on HIGH and then release the pressure quickly.
6. Serve and enjoy!

(Calories 140| Total Fats 6g | Carbs: 9g | Protein 11g| Fiber 1g)

156. Rosemary Potatoes

(Total Time: 35 MIN| Serves: 2)

Ingredients:

- 1 ½ tbsp Butter
- ¾ pound Potatoes, sliced

- 1 Rosemary Sprig
- Salt and Pepper, to taste

Directions:

1. Set the Instant Pot to SAUTE and melt the butter inside.
2. Add the potato slices and cook for 10 minutes, stirring occasionally.
3. Pour the broth over and add the rosemary sprig.
4. Cook on HIGH for a few minutes, 3-4 are enough.
5. Do a quick pressure release.
6. Season with some salt and pepper.
7. Serve and enjoy!

(Calories 175| Total Fats 4g | Carbs: 27g | Protein 4g| Fiber 5g)

157. Eggplant and Spinach Side

(Total Time: 15 MIN| Serves: 2)

Ingredients:

- 1 tbsp Coconut Oil
- ¼ tsp Pepper
- 2 cups cubed Eggplant
- ¼ cup Coconut Milk
- 1 tsp Five Spice Powder
- 1 cups Spinach
- 1 cup Veggie Broth
- 1/4 tsp Salt

Directions:

1. Melt the coconut oil in the Instant Pot on SAUTE.
2. Add the eggplant and cook for a couple of minutes.
3. Stir in the stock and coconut milk.
4. Add the spinach and season with the seasonings.
5. Close the lid and set the IP to MANUAL.
6. Cook for 3 minutes on HIGH.
7. Release the pressure quickly.
8. Serve and enjoy!

(Calories 115| Total Fats 6.5g | Carbs: 8g | Protein 3g| Fiber 1g)

158. Refried Pinto Beans with Cumin

(Total Time: 55 MIN| Serves: 2)

Ingredients:

- 1 cup Water
- 1 cup Veggie Broth
- 1 Jalapeno, diced
- 1 tsp Cumin
- 1/2 pound dried Pinto Beans
- 1 tbsp Butter
- 1 tsp minced Garlic
- ½ tsp Oregano
- ¼ cup diced Onion
- Salt and Pepper, to taste

Directions:

1. Place the beans in a bowl filled with water and let sit for 15 minutes.
2. Drain and rinse them well.
3. Transfer to the IP.
4. Add the rest of the ingredients.
5. Stir well to combine and close the lid.
6. Choose the BEAN/CHILI cooking mode.
7. Cook for 25 minutes.
8. Do a natural pressure release.
9. Blend the mixture with a hand blender.
10. Serve and enjoy!

(Calories 240| Total Fats 9g | Carbs: 35g | Protein 13g|

Fiber 14g)

159. Squash Spaghetti

(Total Time: 20 MIN| Serves: 2)

Ingredients:

- ½ Winter Squash
- 1 ½ cups Water

Directions:

1. Discard the seeds of the squash and place it in the steamer basket.
2. Pour the water into the IP and lower the basket.

3. Close the lid and cook for 6 minutes on HIGH.
4. Do a quick pressure release.
5. Grab a fork and pull of the flesh to make spaghetti-like strings.
6. Serve and enjoy!

(Calories 180| Total Fats 3g | Carbs: 39g | Protein 1g| Fiber 4g)

160. Cauliflower Rice

(Total Time: 25 MIN| Serves: 2)

Ingredients:

- ½ Cauliflower Head
- 1 tbsp Olive Oil
- 1 ½ cups Water
- Pinch of Garlic Powder
- Pinch of Turmeric
- Pinch of Cumin
- 1/4 tsp Salt

Directions:

1. Pour the water into the IP.
2. Chop the cauliflower and place in the steamer basket.
3. Lower the basket into the IP and close the lid.
4. Cook on STEAM for 2 minutes.
5. Do a quick pressure release.
6. Transfer to a food processor along with the remaining ingredients.

7. Pulse until ground.
8. Serve and enjoy!

(Calories 40| Total Fats 0g | Carbs: 2g | Protein 2g| Fiber 2.2g)

161. Garbanzo Mash

(Total Time: 20 MIN| Serves: 2)

Ingredients:

- 1 ¼ cup Garbanzo Beans
- 2 ½ tbsp toasted Pumpkin Seeds
- 1 Garlic Clove
- 1 tsp ground Mustard
- Salt and Pepper, to taste
- Water, as needed

Directions:

1. Place the beans in the IP and add water just enough to cover them.
2. Close the lid and cook on BEAN/CHILI for 10 minutes.
3. Do a quick pressure release.
4. Drain the beans but reserved half of the liquid.
5. Place the beans, the reserved liquid, as well as the remaining ingredients, to a food processor.
6. Pulse until smooth.
7. Season with some salt and pepper.
8. Serve and enjoy!

(Calories 165| Total Fats 8g | Carbs: 26g | Protein 4g| Fiber 3.6g)

162. Paprika and Onion Grits

(Total Time: 15 MIN| Serves: 2)

Ingredients:

- 2/3 cup Quick Cooking Grits
- 1 tbsp Coconut Oil
- ½ Onion, diced
- 1 tsp Paprika
- 2 cups Veggie Broth
- Salt and Pepper, to taste

Directions:

1. Melt the coconut oil in the IP on SAUTE.
2. Add the onions and cook for 3 minutes.
3. Stir in the paprika and grits and cook for an additional minute.
4. Pour the veggie over and stir to combine.
5. Close the lid and cook on HIGH for 6 minutes.
6. Release the pressure quickly.
7. Season with some salt and pepper.
8. Serve and enjoy!

(Calories 200| Total Fats 7g | Carbs: 21g | Protein 3.5g|

Fiber 6.9g)

163. Mashed Potatoes

(Total Time: 15 MIN| Serves: 2)

Ingredients:

- 1 tbsp Coconut Oil
- ¼ cup Milk
- 2 Medium Potatoes
- Pinch of Nutmeg
- ¼ tsp Salt
- Pinch of Pepper
- Water, as needed

Directions:

1. Peel the potatoes and place them inside your Instant Pot.
2. Add just enough water to cover them.
3. Close the lid and choose MANUAL.
4. Cook for 8 minutes on HIGH.
5. Do a quick pressure release.
6. Mash with a potato masher or a hand blend and stir in the remaining ingredients.
7. Serve and enjoy!

(Calories 206| Total Fats 7.2g | Carbs: 34g | Protein 4g|

Fiber 5g)

164. French Onion Brown Rice

(Total Time: 25 MIN| Serves: 2)

Ingredients:

- ¾ cup Veggie Stock
- 1 cup Brown Rice
- 1 cup French Onion Soup
- 1 Butter Stick

Directions:

1. Place all of the ingredients in the IP.
2. Stir well to combine and close the lid.
3. Cook for 20 minutes on HIGH.
4. Do a quick pressure release.
5. Serve and enjoy!

(Calories 400| Total Fats 25g | Carbs: 72g | Protein 9g|

Fiber 21g)

165. Black Bean Dip

(Total Time: 30 MIN| Serves: 2)

Ingredients:

- ¼ pound Black Beans, soaked overnight
- 1 tbsp Olive Oil
- 1/3 cup Tomatoes, chopped
- ¼ tsp Garlic Powder
- 1 ½ tsp Garam Masala Powder
- ¼ cup diced Red Onions
- ¼ tsp Salt
- ½ tsp Chili Powder
- 2 ½ cups Water

Directions:

1. Add the black beans to the IP and pour the water over.
2. Close the lid and cook on BEAN/CHILI for 12 minutes.
3. Do a quick pressure release.
4. Drain the beans and transfer them to a food processor.
5. Wipe the IP clean and heat the oil in it.
6. Add the onions and spices and cook for 2 minutes.
7. Add tomatoes and cook for another 2 minutes.
8. Transfer the mixture to the food processor.
9. Pulse until smooth.
10. Serve and enjoy!

(Calories 220| Total Fats 5g | Carbs: 35g | Protein 2g| Fiber 14g)

166. Spinach and Tofu Mayo Dip

(Total Time: 15 MIN| Serves: 2)

Ingredients:

- ½ cup Tofu
- 3 ounces Spinach
- 1/3 cup Mayonnaise
- 1 tsp Lemon Juice
- ¼ tsp Lemon Zest
- ¼ tsp Salt
- 1 cup Water
- ¼ tsp Dill

Directions:

1. Pour the water into the IP and lower the trivet.
2. Combine all of the ingredients in a baking dish that can fit into the IP.
3. Wrap the dish in foil and place on the trivet.
4. Close the lid and cook for 8 minutes on STEAM.
5. Do a quick pressure release.
6. Blend with a hand blender.
7. Serve and enjoy!

(Calories 94| Total Fats 8g | Carbs: 5g | Protein 1g| Fiber 1g)

167. Mustardy Polenta Bites

(Total Time: 50 MIN| Serves: 2)

Ingredients:

- 1 tsp Dijon Mustard
- ½ dry Polenta
- 1 ½ cups Water
- Pinch of Salt
- Pinch of Pepper

Directions:

1. Pour the water into the IP.
2. Stir in the polenta and cover the lid.
3. Cook on POULTRY for 9 minutes.
4. Release the pressure naturally.
5. Stir in the mustard and spices.
6. Pour in a baking dish and place in the fridge for 30 minutes to set.
7. Cut into squares or serve polenta scoops instead.
8. Enjoy!

(Calories 180| Total Fats 5g | Carbs: 31g | Protein 3g|

Fiber 8g)

168. Appetizer Meatballs

(Total Time: 25 MIN| Serves: 2)

Ingredients:

- ¼ pound ground Meat
- ¼ cup diced Onions
- 2 tbsp Grape Jelly
- ½ tsp Mustard
- 1 tsp Cornstarch
- ½ tsp minced Garlic
- ¼ cup Breadcrumbs
- 2 tbsp Chili Sauce
- 1 cup Water
- 1 tsp Sugar

Directions:

1. Whisk together the water, sugar, chili sauce, grape jelly, cornstarch, and mustard in the IP.
2. Cook on SAUTE until thickened.
3. Meanwhile, combine the rest of the ingredients in a bowl.
4. Make meatballs out of the mixture and place the in the IP.
5. Close the lid and cook on HIGH for 12 minutes.
6. Do a quick pressure release.
7. Serve and enjoy!

(Calories 25| Total Fats 7g | Carbs: 21g | Protein 18g| Fiber 3g)

169. Sweet Potato and Pineapple Chunks

(Total Time: 25 MIN| Serves: 2)

Ingredients:

- 1 pound Sweet Potato Chunks
- 2 tbsp Pineapple Juice
- 2 tbsp Butter
- 1 ½ cup Water
- Pinch of Cinnamon
- Pinch of Nutmeg

Directions:

1. Pour the water into the IP and place the potatoes inside.
2. Close the lid and cook on HIGH for 7 minutes.
3. Do a quick pressure release.
4. Drain the potatoes and transfer to a bowl.
5. Wipe the IP clean and place the remaining ingredients.
6. Cook on SAUTE until the butter is melted and everything is well incorporated.
7. Drizzle the mixture over the potatoes.
8. Serve and enjoy!

(Calories 240| Total Fats 5g | Carbs: 48 g | Protein 4g|

Fiber 7g)

170. Gingery Honey Walnut Snack

(Total Time: 20 MIN| Serves: 2)

Ingredients:

- 1 ¼ cup Walnut Halves
- 1/3 cup Honey
- ½ tsp mince Ginger
- Pinch of Cinnamon
- ¼ cup Water

Directions:

1. Combine all of the ingredients in the Instant Pot.
2. Close the lid and choose SOUP.
3. Cook for 10 minutes.
4. Do a quick pressure release.
5. If the liquid hasn't evaporated, cook o SAUTE until it does.
6. Serve and enjoy!

(Calories 175| Total Fats 4g | Carbs: 37g | Protein 32g| Fiber 4g)

171. Cheesy and Chili Chickpea Dip

(Total Time: 30 MIN| Serves: 2)

Ingredients:

- ½ cup Chickpeas, soaked overnight and drained

- ¼ cup shredded Swiss Cheese
- 2 tbsp Cream Cheese
- 1 Jalapeno Pepper, seeded and diced
- ½ Bell Pepper, chopped
- Salt and Pepper, to taste

Directions:

1. Place the chickpeas in the Instant Pot.
2. Add water to cover them by 3 inches.
3. Close the lid and cook on RICE for 19 minutes.
4. Do a quick pressure release and transfer to a food processor along with the other ingredients.
5. Pulse until smooth.
6. Serve and enjoy!

(Calories 180| Total Fats 9g | Carbs: 18g | Protein 8g|

Fiber 3.5g)

172. Boiled Peanuts

(Total Time: 70 MIN| Serves: 2)

Ingredients:

- 1 tsp Cajun Seasoning
- ¼ pound Raw Peanuts
- 1 tbsp Sea Salt
- Water, as needed

Directions:

1. Clean the peanuts and remove any roots or twigs.

2. Place them in the Instant Pot.
3. Pour enough water to cover.
4. Stir in the salt.
5. Close the lid and cook for 55 minutes on HIGH.
6. Do a natural pressure release.
7. Sprinkle with Cajun.
8. Serve and enjoy!

(Calories 100| Total Fats 10g | Carbs: 8g | Protein 7g| Fiber 2g)

173. Scalloped Potatoes

(Total Time: 15 MIN| Serves: 2)

Ingredients:

- 1 2 tsp Potato Starch
- 2 Potatoes, peeled and sliced
- 1 tsp chopped Chives
- 1 cup Chicken Broth
- 2 tbsp Milk
- 2 tbsp Sour Cream
- ¼ tsp Salt

Directions:

1. Combine the salt, broth, chives, and potatoes, in the Instant Pot.
2. Close the lid and cook for 5 minutes on HIGH.
3. Do a quick pressure release and transfer the potatoes to a plate.

4. Wipe the IP clean and stir in the milk, sour cream, and starch.
5. Cook for 2 minutes.
6. Drizzle the mixture over the potatoes.
7. Serve and enjoy!

(Calories 170| Total Fats 3g | Carbs: 30g | Protein 4g| Fiber 6g)

174. Hot Wings

(Total Time: 20 MIN| Serves: 2)

Ingredients:

- 1 pound Chicken Wings
- 3 tbsp Butter
- 1 tsp Sugar
- 1 tsp Worcestershire Sauce
- ¼ cup Hot Sauce
- 6 ounces Water

Directions:

1. Pour the water into the IP and lower the trivet.
2. Place the wings on the trivet and close the lid.
3. Cook on HIGH for 5 minutes.
4. Meanwhile, combine the remaining ingredients in a bowl.
5. Do a quick pressure release.
6. Wipe the IP clean and return the wings to the pot.
7. Pour the sauce over.

8. Cook on SAUTE until sticky.
9. Serve and enjoy!

(Calories 400| Total Fats 22g| Carbs: 4g | Protein 60g|

Fiber 1g)

175. Carrots in Prosciutto Blankets

(Total Time: 25 MIN| Serves: 2)

Ingredients:

- 1/3 pound Carrots
- 3 ounces Prosciutto, sliced
- 1/3 tsp Paprika
- Pinch of Garlic Powder
- 1 tbsp Olive Oil
- ¼ cup Chicken Stock
- Pinch of Pepper

Directions:

1. Combine the herbs and spices and sprinkle over the carrots.
2. Wrap each carrot in a prosciutto slice.
3. Set your Instant Pot to SAUTE and heat the oil in it.
4. Place the wrapped carrots inside and cook on SAUTE until the prosciutto becomes crispy.
5. Pour the broth over and close the lid.
6. Cook on HIGH for 2 minutes.
7. Do a quick pressure release.

8. Serve and enjoy!

(Calories 145| Total Fats 11g | Carbs: 8g | Protein 4g| Fiber 2g)

176. Mac and Cheese Snack

(Total Time: 17 MIN| Serves: 2)

Ingredients:

- 4 ounces Macaroni
- 1/3 cup shredded Monterrey Jack Cheese
- 1 cup Water

Directions:

1. Combine the water and macaroni in the Instant Pot.
2. Close the lid and set it to RICE.
3. Cook for 5 minutes.
4. Do a quick pressure release.
5. Stir in half of the cheese.
6. Divide between two large ramekins and top with the remaining cheese.
7. Place in the IP and cook for one minute, until melted.
8. Serve and enjoy!

(Calories 135| Total Fats 5.5g | Carbs: 15g | Protein 7g|

Fiber 1.3g)

177. Buttery Corn with Cilantro

(Total Time: 10 MIN| Serves: 2)

Ingredients:

- 2 Ears of Shucked Corn
- 3 tbsp Butter
- 1 tbsp minced Cilantro
- ¼ tsp Salt
- 1 ½ cups Water

Directions:

1. Combine the water and corn in the IP.
2. Cook on HIGH for 4 minutes.
3. Do a quick pressure release.
4. Drain the IP and wipe it clean.
5. Melt the butter in it on SAUTE.
6. Stir in cilantro and salt.
7. Drizzle the butter over the corn.
8. Serve and enjoy!

(Calories 310| Total Fats 21g | Carbs: 32g | Protein 5g|

Fiber 12g)

178. Instant Hummus

(Total Time: 20 MIN| Serves: 2)

Ingredients:

- ¼ Onion
- 1 tbsp Tahini
- ¼ cup Garbanzo Beans
- 1 tbsp chopped Parsley
- ½ tbsp Soy Sauce
- 1 tbsp dried Soybeans
- Juice of ¼ Lemon
- 1 cup Veggie Broth
- ¼ tsp Garlic Powder

Directions:

1. Combine the broth, soybeans, and garbanzo beans, in the IP.
2. Close and seal the lid and choose MANUAL.
3. Cook for 15 minutes on HIGH pressure.
4. Do a natural pressure release.
5. Drain the beans and save the cooking liquid.
6. Transfer the drained beans to a food processor, along with the remaining ingredients.
7. Blend until smooth and keep adding the reserved liquid to reach the desired consistency. Serve and enjoy!

(Calories 160| Total Fats 6.5g | Carbs: 20.2g | Protein 8g| Fiber 6g)

179. Thyme Fries

(Total Time: 13 MIN| Serves: 2)

Ingredients:

- ½ pound Potatoes, cut into strips
- ½ tbsp dried Thyme
- 1 tsp Olive Oil
- ¼ tsp Garlic Powder
- 1 cup Water

Directions:

1. Place the potatoes, oil, thyme, and garlic powder, in a bowl.
2. Toss to coat well.
3. Transfer to the steamer basket.
4. Pour the water into the IP and lower the basket.
5. Close the lid and cook on HIGH for 3 minutes.
6. Do a quick pressure release.
7. Serve and enjoy!

(Calories 120| Total Fats 1.5g | Carbs: 25g | Protein 2g|

Fiber 3g)

180. Turnip and Potato Lemony Dip

(Total Time: 135 MIN| Serves: 2)

Ingredients:

- 1 ½ tbsp Olive Oil
- 1 small Turnip, cut lengthwise
- 1 small Potato, cut lengthwise
- ¼ tsp Garlic Powder
- 2 tbsp Coconut Milk
- 2 tbsp Lemon Juice
- 1 cup Water

Directions:

1. Pour the water into the IP and lower the rack.
2. Place the potato and turnip halves on the rack.
3. Close the lid and hit MANUAL.
4. Cook on HIGH for 9 minutes.
5. Do a quick pressure release.
6. Transfer to a food processor.
7. Add the rest of the ingredients and pulse until smooth.
8. Refrigerate for 2 hours before serving.
9. Serve and enjoy!

(Calories 156| Total Fats 10g | Carbs: 13g | Protein 1g| Fiber 2g)

181. Steamed Carrot Flowers

(Total Time: 15 MIN| Serves: 2)

Ingredients:

- ½ pound Carrots
- 1 cup Water

Directions:

1. Take a sharp knife and cut about 4-5 roves along the carrots.
2. Cut the carrots into coins and you will get your flowers.
3. Place the carrot flowers into the steamer basket.
4. Pour the water into the IP and lower the basket.
5. Close the lid and select MANUAL.
6. Cook for 4 minutes on LOW.
7. Do a quick pressure release.
8. Serve and enjoy!

(Calories 48| Total Fats 0g | Carbs: 11 g | Protein 1g| Fiber 2g)

182. Pumpkin Snack Bowls

(Total Time: 30 MIN| Serves: 2)

Ingredients:

- 2/3 pounds Pumpkin
- ½ cup Water
- Pinch of Cinnamon
- 1 tbsp Honey
- 1 ½ tbsp Maple Syrup

Directions:

1. Cut the pumpkin in half and discard the seeds.
2. Pour the water into the IP and lower the rack.
3. Place the pumpkin on the rack and close the lid.
4. Cook on HIGH for 13 minutes.
5. Do a quick pressure release.
6. Wait to cool down and scoop out the flesh into a bowl.
7. Add the cinnamon and honey and mash with a potato masher.
8. Transfer to two bowls.
9. Drizzle with maple syrup.
10. Serve and enjoy!

(Calories 140| Total Fats 3g | Carbs: 17g | Protein 2| Fiber 4g)

183. Turmeric Fingerling Potato Sticks

(Total Time: 35 MIN| Serves: 2)

Ingredients:

- 2/3 pound Fingerling Potatoes
- 1 cup Chicken Broth
- 1 tsp Turmeric Powder
- 2 tbsp Butter

Directions:

1. Wash the potatoes, peel them, and cut into strips.
2. Pour the broth into the Instant Pot.
3. Arrange the potatoes in a single rack on the rack, and lower it into the pot.
4. Cook for 5 minutes on HIGH.
5. Do a quick pressure release.
6. Drain the IP and wipe it clean.
7. Melt the butter in the IP on SAUTE and add the turmeric powder.
8. Drizzle the mixture over the potato sticks.
9. Serve and enjoy!

(Calories 180| Total Fats 4g | Carbs: 28g | Protein 4g|

Fiber 3g)

184. Ricotta and Cheddar Veggie Appetizer

(Total Time: 25 MIN| Serves: 2)

Ingredients:

- 1 1/3 cup shredded Cheddar Cheese
- 3 tbsp Ricotta Cheese
- ½ pound Yukon Gold Potatoes, diced
- ½ cup Broccoli Florets
- 1 ½ cups Water
- 1 tbsp Oil
- Salt and Pepper, to taste

Directions:

1. Combine the potatoes, water and broccoli in the IP.
2. Close the lid and cook on HIGH for 4 minutes.
3. Do a quick pressure release.
4. Drain the veggies and wipe the IP clean.
5. Return them to the pot and set it to SAUTE.
6. Stir in the rest of the ingredients and cook until the cheese is melted.
7. Serve and enjoy!

(Calories 178| Total Fats 11g | Carbs: 12g | Protein 7g| Fiber 3g)

185. Coconut Cake

(Total Time: 55 MIN| Serves: 2)

Ingredients:

- 1 Egg, yolk and white separated
- ½ cup Coconut Flour
- 1 tbsp melted Coconut Oil
- ¼ tsp Coconut Extract
- ¾ cup warm Coconut Milk
- ¼ cup Coconut Sugar
- 1 cup Water

Directions:

1. Beat the white until soft form peaks.
2. Bea tin the sugar and yolk.
3. Add the coconut oil and extract and stir to combine.
4. Fold in the coconut flour.
5. Line or grease a small baking dish an pour the batter into it.
6. Pour the water into the IP and lower the trivet.
7. Place the dish on the trivet.
8. Cook for 40 minutes on HIGH.
9. Do a quick pressure release.
10. Serve and enjoy!

(Calories 350| Total Fats 14g | Carbs: 47g | Protein 7g| Fiber 7g)

186. Cherry Pie

(Total Time: 45 MIN| Serves: 2)

Ingredients:

- ¾ Pie Crust, cut in half
- 2 cups Water
- 1 cup pitted Cherries
- 1 ½ tbsp Quick Tapioca
- 1/3 cup Sugar
- ¼ tsp Vanilla Extract
- Pinch of Salt

Directions:

1. Pour the water into the IP and lower the trivet.
2. In a bowl, combine he cherries, extract, sugar, salt and tapioca.
3. Grease a baking dish and place half of the pie crust at the bottom.
4. Pour the filling over.
5. Cut the other pie crust half into strips and arrange over the filling.
6. Place the baking dish on the trivet and close the lid.
7. Cook on HIGH for 14 minutes.
8. Do a quick pressure release. Serve and enjoy!

(Calories 390| Total Fats 12g | Carbs: 70g | Protein 2g|

Fiber 2g)

187. Yogurt Vanilla Lighter Cheesecake

(Total Time: 6 hours and 60 MIN| Serves: 2)

Ingredients:

- 1 small Egg
- ½ cup Yogurt
- ¼ tsp Vanilla
- 2 tbsp melted Butter
- ½ cup Graham Cracker Crumbs
- 2 ounces Cream Cheese, softened
- 1 tbsp Sugar
- 1 cup Water

Directions:

1. Pour the water into the Instant Pot and lower the trivet.
2. Combine the butter and crackers and press the mixture into the bottom of a greased small baking dish.
3. Bea the yogurt, vanilla, sugar, and cream cheese.
4. Beat in the egg.
5. Pour over the crust.
6. Place the baking dish on the trivet and close the id.
7. Cook on HIGH for 20 minutes.
8. Do a quick pressure release.
9. Let cool to room temperature then place it in the fridge for 5-6 hours.
10. Serve and enjoy!

(Calories 280| Total Fats 9g | Carbs: 26g | Protein 6g| Fiber 1g)

188. Pumpkin Pie

(Total Time: 30 MIN| Serves: 2)

Ingredients:

- ½ pound Butternut Squash, diced
- 3 tbsp Honey
- 1 tsp Cornstarch
- ¼ tsp Cinnamon
- ¼ cup Coconut Milk
- 1 small Egg
- 1 cup Water

Directions:

1. Pour the water into the Instant Pot. Lower the trivet.
2. Place the squash on the trivet and close the lid.
3. Cook for 4 minutes on HIGH.
4. Transfer the squash to a plate but let the cooking liquid remain in the IP.
5. Combine the squash with the remaining ingredients in a bowl.
6. Grease a baking dish and pour the batter into it.
7. Place on the trivet and cook for 10 minutes on HIGH.
8. Do a quick pressure release. Serve and enjoy!

(Calories 173| Total Fats 2g | Carbs: 40g | Protein 3g| Fiber 4g)

189. Molten Lava Cake

(Total Time: 20 MIN| Serves: 2)

Ingredients:

- 1 tbsp Butter, melted
- 3 tbsp Almond Flour
- ½ cup chopped Dark Chocolate
- 1 cup Water
- 1 Egg, beaten
- ¼ tsp Vanilla
- ¼ cup Coconut Sugar

Directions:

1. Pour the water into the Instant Pot. Lower the trivet.
2. Combine all of the remaining ingredients in a bowl.
3. Grease two ramekins and divide the batter among them.
4. Place them on the trivet and close the lid.
5. Cook for 9 minutes on HIGH.
6. Do a quick pressure release.
7. Serve and enjoy!

(Calories 414| Total Fats 23g | Carbs: 48g | Protein 8g|

Fiber 2.6g)

190. Stuffed Peaches

(Total Time: 35 MIN| Serves: 2)

Ingredients:

- 2 Peaches
- 2 tbsp Butter
- ¼ tsp Almond Extract
- Pinch of Cinnamon
- 2 tbsp Cassava Flour
- 2 tbsp Maple Syrup
- 2 tsp chopped Almonds
- 1 ½ cups Water

Directions:

1. Pour the water into the Instant Pot. Lower the rack.
2. Slice the tops off the peaches and discard the pits.
3. Combine the rest of the ingredients in a bowl.
4. Stuff the peaches with the mixture.
5. Place them on the rack and close the lid.
6. Cook for 3 minutes on HIGH.
7. Do a quick pressure release.
8. Serve and enjoy!

(Calories 145| Total Fats 5g | Carbs: 25g | Protein 1.5g|

Fiber 1g)

191. Blueberry Jam

(Total Time: 30 MIN| Serves: 2)

Ingredients:

- ¼ cup Honey
- ½ cup Blueberries

Directions:

1. Combine the honey and blueberries in the IP.
2. Set it to KEEP WARM and let it sit until the honey turns liquid.
3. When the honey becomes liquid, set the IP to SAUTE and bring it to a boil.
4. Cover, press CANCEL, and set to MANUAL.
5. Cook on HIGH for 2 minutes.
6. Do a natural pressure release.
7. Serve and enjoy!

(Calories 180| Total Fats 0g | Carbs: 40g | Protein 1g| Fiber 1g)

192. Vanilla Rice Pudding

(Total Time: 30 MIN| Serves: 2)

Ingredients:

- 1/3 cup Basmati Rice
- ½ tsp Vanilla Extract
- ¼ cup Heavy Cream
- 2/3 cup Milk
- 1 ½ tbsp Maple Syrup
- Pinch of Salt

Directions:

1. Combine everything in the Instant Pot, except the cream.
2. Close the lid and set the IP to PORRIDGE.
3. Cook for 17 minutes.
4. Do a natural pressure release.
5. Stir in the heavy cream.
6. Serve and enjoy!

(Calories 240| Total Fats 7g | Carbs: 38g | Protein 5g|

Fiber 7g)

193. Pressure Cooked Brownies

(Total Time: 45 MIN| Serves: 2)

Ingredients:

- 1 tbsp Honey
- 2 cups Water
- ½ cup Sugar
- 1 Egg
- 2 tbsp Cocoa Powder
- Pinch of Salt
- ¼ cup melted Butter
- 2/3 cup Flour
- 1/3 cup Baking Powder

Directions:

1. Pour the water into the Instant Pot. Lower the trivet.
2. Whisk the wet ingredients in one bowl.
3. Stir together the dry ones in another.
4. Combine the two mixtures gently.
5. Grease a baking dish with some cooking spray.
6. Pour the batter into it.
7. Place the dish on the trivet and close the lid.
8. Cook on HIGH for 25 minutes.
9. Do a quick pressure release.
10. Serve and enjoy!

(Calories 525| Total Fats 25g | Carbs: 75g | Protein 8g|

Fiber 3g)

194. Almond Tapioca Pudding

(Total Time: 30 MIN| Serves: 2)

Ingredients:

- 2/3 cup Almond Milk
- ¼ cup Tapioca Pearls
- 2 tbsp Sugar
- ½ tsp Almond Extract
- ½ cup Water
- Pinch of Cinnamon

Directions:

1. Pour the water into the Instant Pot. Lower the trivet.
2. Take a heat –proof bowl and place all of the ingredients into it.
3. Stir well to combine.
4. Cover with a foil and place the bowl on the trivet.
5. Close the lid and set the IP to MANUAL.
6. Cook on HIGH for 7-8 minutes.
7. Do a natural pressure release.
8. Serve and enjoy!

(Calories 190| Total Fats 2.5g | Carbs: 39g | Protein 2.5g| Fiber 5.2g)

195. Blondies with Peanut Butter

(Total Time: 55 MIN| Serves: 2)

Ingredients:

- 1 ½ cups Water
- ¼ cup Brown Sugar
- 2 tbsp White Sugar
- 1/3 cup Oats
- 1/3 cup Flour
- 1 Egg
- 2 tbsp Peanut Butter
- 3 tbsp Butter, softened
- Pinch of Salt

Directions:

1. Pour the water into the Instant Pot. Lower the trivet.
2. Grease a baking dish with cooking spray and set aside.
3. Cream together the sugars, egg, butter, peanut butter, and salt, in a mixing bowl.
4. Fold in the dry ingredients.
5. Pour the batter into the greased pan.
6. Place the pan on the trivet and close the lid.
7. Cook on POULTRY for 26 minutes.
8. Wait 10 minutes before doing a quick pressure release.
9. Let it cool for 15 minutes before inverting onto a plate and slicing.
10. Serve and enjoy!

(Calories 550| Total Fats 18g | Carbs: 61g | Protein 8g| Fiber 1.5g)

196. Chocolate Chip Oat Cookies

(Total Time: 30 MIN| Serves: 2)

Ingredients:

- ¼ cup Oats
- 2 tbsp Milk
- 1 tbsp Honey
- 2 tbsp Sugar
- 2 tsp Coconut Oil
- ½ tsp Vanilla Extract
- 2 tbsp Chocolate Chips
- ¼ cup Flour
- Pinch of Salt
- 1 ½ cups Water

Directions:

1. Pour the water into the Instant Pot. Lower the trivet.
2. Combine all of the cookie ingredients in a bowl.
3. Line a baking dish with parchment paper.
4. With a cookie scoop, drop the cookies onto the paper.
5. Make sure to flatten them slightly.
6. Place the dish on the trivet and close the lid.
7. Set the IP to MANUAL.
8. Cook on HIGH for 8 minutes.
9. Do a quick pressure release.
10. If they are not crispy for your liking.
11. Cook them on SAUTE for a few extra minutes.
12. Serve and enjoy!

(Calories 410| Total Fats 20g | Carbs: 58g | Protein 6g|
Fiber 1g)

197. Banana Chocolate Chip Muffins

(Total Time: 30 MIN| Serves: 2)

Ingredients:

- 1/3 cup Buttermilk
- 1/3 tsp Baking Soda
- 2 tbsp Chocolate Chips
- 1 Banana, mashed
- ½ cup Flour
- 1 cup Water
- 1 tbsp Honey
- Pinch of Cinnamon
- 3 tbsp Butter, melted
- 1 tbsp Flaxseeds

Directions:

1. Pour the water into the Instant Pot. Lower the trivet.
2. Whisk together all of the ingredients.
3. Make sure to get rid of all the lumps.
4. Divide the mixture between two silicone muffin cups.
5. Place the muffin cups on the trivet.
6. Close the lid and set the IP to MANUAL.
7. Cook on HIGH for 15 minutes.
8. Do a quick pressure release.
9. Serve and enjoy!

(Calories 230| Total Fats 13g | Carbs: 30g | Protein 3g|

Fiber 3g)

198. Simple Vanilla Egg Custard

(Total Time: 25 MIN| Serves: 2)

Ingredients:

- 2 Eggs
- Pinch of Cinnamon
- ¼ tsp Vanilla Extract
- 1 1/3 cup Milk
- 1 ½ cups Water
- ¼ cup Sugar

Directions:

1. Pour the water into the Instant Pot. Lower the trivet.
2. In a bowl, beat the eggs.
3. Add the rest of the ingredients and whisk to combine.
4. Grease 2 ramekins and divide the mixture between them.
5. Place the ramekins on the trivet and close the lid.
6. Cook on HIGH for 7 minutes.
7. Release the pressure naturally.
8. Serve and enjoy!

(Calories 150| Total Fats g | Carbs: 16g | Protein 7g| Fiber 1g)

199. Chocolate Fondue

(Total Time: 15 MIN| Serves: 2)

Ingredients:

- 5 ounces Chocolate
- Pinch of Cinnamon
- 4 ounces Heavy Cream
- 1 tsp Coconut Liqueur
- Pinch of Salt
- ½ cup Lukewarm Water

Directions:

1. Pour the water into the Instant Pot. Lower the trivet.
2. Melt the chocolate in a microwave, in a heatproof bowl.
3. Add the rest of the ingredients, except the liqueur, and stir to combine.
4. Place the dish on the trivet.
5. Close and seal the lid and set the IP to STEAM.
6. Cook for 4 minutes.
7. Add the liqueur, stir to incorporate.
8. Serve and enjoy!

(Calories 215| Total Fats 20g | Carbs: 12g | Protein 2g|

Fiber 0g)

200. Gingery Applesauce

(Total Time: 15 MIN| Serves: 2)

Ingredients:

- 1 ½ pounds Apples, chopped
- 1 ½ tbsp Crystalized Ginger
- ½ cup Water

Directions:

1. Pour the water into the Instant Pot.
2. Add the apples and ginger and stir to combine.
3. Close the lid and set the IP to MANUAL.
4. Cook on HIGH for 4 minutes.
5. Wait 10 minutes and then release the pressure naturally.
6. Msh with a potato masher.
7. Serve and enjoy!

(Calories 260| Total Fats 1g | Carbs: 66g | Protein 5g|

Fiber 5g)

201. Peach Crumb

(Total Time: 55 MIN| Serves: 2)

Ingredients:

- ¼ cup Breadcrumbs
- 2 small Peaches, sliced
- 2 tbsp Lemon Juice
- ¼ tsp Lemon Zest
- ¼ cup melted Butter
- ¼ tsp ground Ginger
- Pinch of Cinnamon
- 2 tbsp Sugar
- 1 ½ cups Water

Directions:

1. Pour the water into the Instant Pot. Lower the trivet.
2. Grease a baking dish with cooking spray and arrange the peach slices in it.
3. Combine the remaining ingredients in a bowl and spread over the peaches.
4. Place the dish on the trivet and close the lid.
5. Cook on HIGH for 20 minutes.
6. Do a natural pressure release.
7. Serve and enjoy!

(Calories 505| Total Fats 25g | Carbs: 70g | Protein 2.5g| Fiber 4g)

202. Pear Ricotta Cake

(Total Time: 30 MIN| Serves: 2)

Ingredients:

- 2 tbsp Sugar
- 1 Egg
- 1 Pear, diced
- ½ cup Ricotta
- ½ cup Flour
- ½ tsp Baking Soda
- ½ tsp Vanilla
- 1 ½ tbsp Oil
- 1 tbsp Lemon Juice
- 1 tsp Baking Powder
- 2 cups Water

Directions:

1. Pour the water into the Instant Pot. Lower the trivet.
2. Whisk together all of the ingredients in a large bowl.
3. Stir well to avoid leaving any lumos.
4. Grease a baking dish that fits inside the IP, with some cooking spray.
5. Pour the batter into the dish and then place it on the trivet.
6. Close the lid of the IP and set it to MANUAL.
7. Cook on HIGH for 15 minutes.
8. Release the pressure quickly.
9. Serve and enjoy!

(Calories 452| Total Fats 20g | Carbs: 60g | Protein 13g| Fiber 4g)

203. Lemon and Blackberry Compote

(Total Time: 135 MIN| Serves: 2)

Ingredients:

- Juice of ½ Lemon
- Pinch of Lemon Zest
- 1 cup Frozen Blackberries
- 5 tbsp Sugar
- 1 tbsp Cornstarch
- 1 tbsp Water

Directions:

1. Combine the lemon juice, sugar, zest, and blackberries, in your IP.
2. Close the lid and set the IP to MANUAL.
3. Cook for 3 minutes on HIGH.
4. Do a natural pressure release.
5. Whisk together the water and cornstarch and stir the mixture into the compote.
6. Cook on SAUTE until slightly thickened.
7. Place in the fridge for 1 ½ - 2 hours.
8. Serve and enjoy!

(Calories 220 | Total Fats 0g | Carbs: 60g | Protein 1g|

Fiber 4g)

204. Poached Gingery Orange Pears

(Total Time: 20 MIN| Serves: 2)

Ingredients:

- 2 Pears
- 1 cup Orange Juice
- 1 tsp minced Ginger
- Pinch of Nutmeg
- Pinch of Cinnamon
- 2 tbsp Sugar

Directions:

1. Pour the juice into the IP.
2. Stir in the sugar, ginger, cinnamon, and nutmeg.
3. Peel the pears and cut in half.
4. Place the inside the IP.
5. Close the lid and cook for 7 minutes on HIGH.
6. Do a natural pressure release.
7. Serve drizzled with the sauce.
8. Enjoy!

(Calories 170| Total Fats 1g | Carbs: 43g | Protein 1g| Fiber 5g)

205. Caramel Flan

(Total Time: 30 MIN| Serves: 2)

Ingredients:

- 1 Egg
- 4 ounces Condensed Milk
- ½ cup Coconut Milk
- ½ tsp Vanilla Extract
- 1 ½ cups plus 3 tbsp Water
- 5 tbsp Sugar

Directions:

1. Combine the sugar and water in the IP on SAUTE.
2. Cook until caramelized.
3. Divide the caramelized sugar (immediately otherwise it will harden) between 2 greased ramekins.
4. Bea the remaining ingredients in a bowl and then pour on top of the caramel.
5. Cover with aluminum foil.
6. Pour the water into the Instant Pot. Lower the trivet.
7. Place the ramekins on the trivet and close the lid.
8. Cook on HIGH for 5 minutes.
9. Do a natural pressure release.
10. Allow to cool before inverting onto a plate.
11. Serve and enjoy!

(Calories 108| Total Fats 3g | Carbs: 16g | Protein 3g| Fiber 0g)

Conclusion

Although many of these recipes will surely leave you some leftovers for you to much on later, they are all perfectly designed to fit two grown tummies. Rest assured that you will not leave your dinner table with your rumbling gut.

Did you like these recipes? Leave a review on Amazon and let the other pressure cookers know. Your feedback is always greatly appreciated.

Thank you!

CPSIA information can be obtained
at www.ICGtesting.com
Printed in the USA
LVHW050207220523
747655LV00011B/577

9 781983 961663